Dead Man's Shoes

This is a work of fiction. All of the characters, events, and organizations portrayed in this work are either products of the authors' imagination or used fictitiously.

Dead Man's Shoes
Copyright © 2011 by Joseph Zettelmaier

All rights reserved. No part of this book may be reproduced in any form by any electronic or mechanical means including photocopying, recording, or information storage and retrieval without permission in writing from the author.

ISBN-13: 978-0692563267
ISBN-10: 0692563261

For information about production rights, visit:
www.jzettelmaier.com

Published by Sordelet Ink
Cover by David Blixt

Dead Man's Shoes

A PLAY BY
JOSEPH ZETTELMAIER

Published by
Sordelet Ink

Dead Man's Shoes premiered as a co-production between Williamston Theatre (Williamston, MI) and the Performance Network Theatre (Ann Arbor, MI). It opened at Williamston Theatre on January 26, 2014. The production was directed by David Wolber. Set Design by Kirk Domer. Costume Design by Amber Marisa Cook. Lighting Design by Daniel C. Walker. Sound Design by Will Myers. Prop Design by Stefanie Din. Technical Direction by Ed Weingart. The production was stage managed by Rochelle Clark.

The cast was as follows:

>INJUN BILL PICOTE: Drew Parker
>FROGGY: Aral Basil Gribble II
>ACTOR 1: Paul Hopper
>ACTOR 2: Maggie Meyer

"The Ballad of Injun Bill" - Lyrics by Joseph Zettelmaier. Original music by Rochelle Clark and John Natiw.

NOTE: It is the playwright's intention that each production can compose their own music around the lyrics, as best suits the production.

Dead Man's Shoes was the recipient of an Edgerton Foundation New American Play Award in 2013.

Cast of Characters

INJUN BILL PICOTE, 35, an outlaw
FROGGY, 30s, an army cook
ACTOR 1: SHERIFF, MADAME FLORA, ABEL, DEATH
ACTOR 2: SISTER BERNADETTE, BELLE, BJARMA, MARTHA

Time
1883

Place
Various locales in the Western United States

ACT I

Scene 1

(ACTORS 1 and 2 are illuminated. They speak the first part of the ballad out loud)

ACTOR 1
Gather 'round, all you sinners
And tall-tale spinners
Gather 'round, all you trav'lers
And sit for a spell

ACTOR 2
Let the fire here warm you
While we players inform you
Of a black-hearted scoundrel
Come straight out of Hell

ACTOR 1
T'was a murderous liar
Who ate coal and crapped fire

ACTOR 2
With a belly for vengeance
He never could fill

ACTOR 1
AND HE WANDERED THE WEST
DOIN' WHAT HE DID BEST

ACTOR 2
THE VILLAINOUS OUTLAW
THEY CALLED INJUN BILL.

(The music plays. ACTOR 1 sings)

ACTOR 1
IN A DARK AND RUN-DOWN PRISON
IN THE HEART OF NORTH DAKOTA
SAT THE SON OF THE LAKOTA
WITH THE DEVIL IN HIS EYES
HE SPENT TWO YEARS IN THE SADDLE
FIGHTIN' HIS OWN PRIVATE BATTLE
AND IT LANDED HIM IN JAIL,
ONE STEP FURTHER FROM HIS PRIZE

INJUN BILL, INJUN BILL
THINK ON THIS BEFORE YOU SLAUGHTER
EVERY GIRL IS SOMEONE'S DAUGHTER,
EVERY MAN IS SOMEONE'S SON
INJUN BILL, INJUN BILL
LET YOUR BETTER ANGELS GUIDE YOU
'CAUSE THE DEVIL THAT'S INSIDE YOU
WANTS HIS DUE BEFORE IT'S DONE

(Lights rise. A prison in North Dakota. It's dirty & dark. There are two cells, with bars separating them. In one sits INJUN BILL PICOTE, a hat over his face making it unclear if he's sleeping or not. In the other is FROGGY, playing a harmonica. He is a large man with a moustache wearing a ragged shirt, a forage cap & military pants. FROGGY finishes his song. After a moment--)

INJUN BILL
Don't stop.

(Beat. FROGGY just stares at him)

INJUN BILL
I said don't stop. *(Beat)* You deaf and ugly, or just ugly?

(Beat. FROGGY laughs at that)

FROGGY
You a funny som'bitch, ain'tcha?

(INJUN BILL shrugs)

FROGGY
In there for two days, you ain't said one word. Hell, you farted in your sleep and I thought we was about to have a conversation. Sittin' there for two days and all you gots to say is "Don't stop?"

INJUN BILL
This isn't a social club.

FROGGY
Just a neighborly howdy-do is all I ask.

(INJUN BILL says nothing)

FROGGY
What'cha in for?

INJUN BILL
Being sloppy.

FROGGY
That's a crime? Shit, I been sloppy since I came outta my momma.

INJUN BILL
Got drunk. Got caught.

FROGGY
Gettin' tore up ain't a crime.

INJUN BILL
Cut a man up.

FROGGY
That a fact?

INJUN BILL
It is.

FROGGY
Yeah, I can see the law frownin' on that. What'd he do?

INJUN BILL
Wore the wrong shoes.

(Beat)

FROGGY
Huh. Wrong shoes?

INJUN BILL
That's right.

FROGGY
I reckon I don't follow.

INJUN BILL
Not my concern.

FROGGY
You carved some poor som'bitch up 'cause he was wearing the wrong shoes?

INJUN BILL
Would've been worse if he was wearin' the right ones.

FROGGY
Mister, I can't quite decide if you're crazy or just puttin' me on.

INJUN BILL
That's not my concern either.

FROGGY
My gut tells me "crazy". And I'm a man who goes with his gut.

INJUN BILL
Obviously.

(Beat)

FROGGY
You sayin' I'm fat?

INJUN BILL
You're saying you're fat. I'm just seeing it.

FROGGY
Why don't you smart-ass your way over here and say that to my face?

INJUN BILL
Nope.

FROGGY
You gutless?

INJUN BILL
I just wanted to hear more mouth-harp. You gonna play or not?

(FROGGY lifts his leg and farts)

FROGGY
That's a song I wrote special, just for you.

(Beat. INJUN BILL gets deadly serious)

INJUN BILL
Where you get your shoes?

(Beat)

FROGGY
What?

INJUN BILL
See them things on your feet? Those are shoes. Where'd you get 'em?

FROGGY
(Crossing to the bars) Your mama give 'em to me for a job well-done.

(With surprising speed, INJUN BILL runs to the bars and grabs FROGGY's ankles, tips FROGGY over, and pulls off his shoes. FROGGY squeals with fear)

FROGGY
AH! AH! Save me, Jesus! This som'bitch gonna cut off my feet!

(The SHERIFF walks in as INJUN BILL examines the shoes)

SHERIFF
Hey! People are trying to sleep here!

FROGGY
Sheriff, that som'bitch stole my shoes and tried to....

SHERIFF
Oh fer... just give him his shoes back already.

INJUN BILL
Make me.

FROGGY
Yeah! Make him!

SHERIFF
(Lowering his head) I tell ya, after everything we've been through, havin' you as my guests these past days... I had hoped you'd find yourselves more agreeable.

FROGGY
I want another cell.

SHERIFF
Ain't got one. *(Sits)* "If you chase two rabbits, you shall catch neither." That's a Russian proverb, ladies. Means if you want too much, you wind up with nothin' at all.

FROGGY
You sure that's...?

SHERIFF
I'm a student of philosophy myself. Somethin' about swimmin' through the great minds of the past, seein' how they reflect upon these times we live in... makes me feel a certain... connectedness. For example... *(He rises, crosses towards them)* You men...you in dire circumstances.

FROGGY
We ain't even gone to trial yet!

SHERIFF
Surely, surely. But 'round here, not many do. Fella gets a drunk on, gets a lynch mob rollin'... and I'm just one man here, ladies. If they come to hang ya, I'm not likely to stop them.

FROGGY
WHAT?!

SHERIFF
This is my conundrum. For reasons passing all logic, I've taken something of a shine to you two butt-flaps. I look at you, and I see the failure of the human condition. And I'm reminded of something Hippocrates said. "Extreme remedies are appropriate for extreme diseases."

FROGGY
We ain't sick!

SHERIFF
A hangin' won't help you boys, so I ask myself... what would prove an effective remedy?

FROGGY
Lettin' us go?

SHERIFF
Nothing short of a sign from God would possess me to do that.

FROGGY
Then at least put me somewhere else! I don't wanna be next to this foot-cuttin' som'bitch.

SHERIFF
Pigs don't wanna sleep in shit, and yet they do. You think on that.

(A knock at the door)

MABEL
(offstage) Sheriff!

SHERIFF
Ladies, if you'll excuse me. What is it, Mabel?

(He leaves)

FROGGY
You gonna try to kill me again?

INJUN BILL
Didn't try to kill you before.

FROGGY
I was just trying to make conversation before. You didn't have to get all surly.

INJUN BILL
I don't care.

FROGGY
I feel like we got off on the wrong foot. *(Beat)* Yep. The wrong foot. *(Beat)* Can I have my shoes back?

(INJUN BILL tosses him his shoes. FROGGY inspects them)

FROGGY
You sure these are my shoes?

INJUN BILL
Yep.

FROGGY
'Cause I can't see real good in the dark.

INJUN BILL
Yep.

FROGGY
I ain't so sure.

INJUN BILL
I don't care.

FROGGY
I'm real familiar with my odors. These don't smell

right.

INJUN BILL
(Temper rising) Who's shoes you think they are, jackass? It's just you and me here!

FROGGY
Coulda give me your shoes.

INJUN BILL
Why. Would I do that?

FROGGY
'Cause... um... 'cause my shoes are better?

(INJUN BILL walks to the bars, puts his boot up)

INJUN BILL
These are genuine shitkickers! What you got are two snot-rags tied 'round a sole! So why don't you shut the fuck up and...!

(FROGGY runs over, grabs INJUN BILL's boot, and flips him over. INJUN BILL lies there for a long time saying nothing. Finally--)

INJUN BILL
Reckon I had that coming.

FROGGY
Reckon you did.

INJUN BILL
Yep.

FROGGY
You ain't mad?

INJUN BILL
Should be. But I ain't.

FROGGY
Why not? *(He thinks about it)*

INJUN BILL
Hmmm.

(The SHERIFF enters, excited and carrying a telegram)

SHERIFF
Ladies... I... huh... I got a situation. This here telegram says... ah.... *(He drops the keys just out of the men's reach)* Best of luck! *(He giggles excitedly then bolts out the door)*

(FROGGY and INJUN BILL stare at the keys)

FROGGY
What the hell was that?

INJUN BILL
No idea.

FROGGY
Them the keys?

INJUN BILL
Looks like it.

FROGGY
All right then.

(They both dive for them, but neither can quite reach)

FROGGY
C'mere you rat bastards.... *(Manages to grab them)* Yes! Oh sweet merciful Jesus yes!!

*(He frees himself. He then runs straight out the door. INJUN BILL just watches him, expression-

less. FROGGY returns)

FROGGY
Say you're sorry.

INJUN BILL
What?

FROGGY
Say you're sorry that you almost cut my feet off.

INJUN BILL
I didn't almost cut your feet off.

FROGGY
Just say it.

(INJUN BILL says nothing)

FROGGY
S-A-R-Y. Say it.

(INJUN BILL says nothing)

FROGGY
Som'bitch.

(FROGGY opens his cell. INJUN BILL just stands there)

FROGGY
I reckon we should leave before the Sheriff changes his mind.

INJUN BILL
I reckon.

(They run out of the jail. Lights fade)

Scene 2

ACTOR 2
(singing)
THE OUTLAW CAVES HE HID IN
HELD HIS TREASURE AND HIS MEM'RIES
OF DEAD FRIENDS AND DEADER ENEMIES,
AND THE TALES HIS KNIVES WOULD TELL
AND HE THOUGHT OF OLD GEORGE PARROT
'TIL HIS HEART JUST WOULDN'T BEAR IT
'CAUSE HE KNEW THEY'D NEVER MEET AGAIN,
'CEPT AT THE GATES OF HELL

(A cave in Rattlesnake Butte, North Dakota. FROGGY inspects it while INJUN BILL goes through some supplies)

FROGGY
Good lord, I coulda had a compass, two hounds, and a map tattooed to my hand, I still wouldn't have found this cave.

INJUN BILL
I been here before.

FROGGY
This a hide-out?

INJUN BILL
It is.

FROGGY
That make you some kinda outlaw, then?

INJUN BILL
It does.

FROGGY
No shit?

INJUN BILL
No shit.

FROGGY
What's your name?

(INJUN BILL says nothing, inspecting a belt full of knives)

FROGGY
We been on the road two hours now. Reckon I should know your name.

(INJUN BILL finds a military saber, examines it)

FROGGY
They call me Froggy.

INJUN BILL
That's fine.

FROGGY
On account of my Christian name.

INJUN BILL
Mm-hmm.

FROGGY
Jean-Phillipe DeLaRoux Baptiste.

(Beat)

INJUN BILL
I get it.

FROGGY
Born in Baton Rouge. Formerly of the 7th Cavalry, under General Custer hisself.

INJUN BILL
Mm-hmmm.

FROGGY
So... what do they call you, fella?

(Beat)

INJUN BILL
Bill.

FROGGY
Bill?

INJUN BILL
Bill.

FROGGY
That don't sound like no outlaw name.

INJUN BILL
That's not my concern.

FROGGY
You should be somethin' like "Bloody Bill" or "Bill the... Bloody" or somethin' like that.

INJUN BILL
Don't care what I should be.

FROGGY
Jesus, you a tight-lipped som'bitch. You got a last name, Unimpressive Bill?

(Beat. His last name is pronounced PEE-coat)

INJUN BILL
Picote.

FROGGY
(That sinks in) Smack my ass! You're Injun Bill Picote?!

INJUN BILL
Bill.

FROGGY
All this time, I've been talking to Injun Bill Picote?

INJUN BILL
I reckon.

FROGGY
Smack my ass!

INJUN BILL
No.

FROGGY
I heard you was in jail.

INJUN BILL
I was. With you.

FROGGY
No, no. I mean… didn't they catch you in Montana or somethin'?

INJUN BILL
Caught the gang I rode with. Didn't catch me. At

least, not then.

FROGGY
Goddamn, son. You're famous.

INJUN BILL
I am?

FROGGY
Well, with some folks. I heard you was the deadliest man alive with a knife.

INJUN BILL
There's probably deadlier.

FROGGY
Heard you put a man's eye out at a hundred paces for calling your mama a bean-eater.

INJUN BILL
My mother was Lakota.

FROGGY
I figured it was something like that. What with you bein' Injun Bill and all. *(Beat)* Wait. You say "Lakota?"

INJUN BILL
Mm-hmm.

(Beat)

FROGGY
What you need to understand is… I was just Custer's cook, alright? I never went on no battle field, and I never killed me no injun. Redskin. Lakota.

INJUN BILL
Fine.

FROGGY
So don't cut off my scalp or...

INJUN BILL
I ain't gonna kill you.

FROGGY
You sure about that?

INJUN BILL
You ain't wearin' the right shoes.

FROGGY
So I gotta ask. What's your hitch when it comes to a man's shoes?

INJUN BILL
Lemme ask you somethin'. Why are you still here?

FROGGY
Huh?

INJUN BILL
We busted out two hours back. Why ain't you shoved off?

FROGGY
Oh. I just... um... do you want me to go?

INJUN BILL
Yep.

FROGGY
Oh. OK. I understand.

INJUN BILL
Good.

FROGGY
You don't want me around.

INJUN BILL
Yep.

FROGGY
Fine! I don't need to follow around no half-injun foot-cutter!

INJUN BILL
Good. Go back to Louisiana.

FROGGY
Like this? Nossir. I gotta make my way. Then I'll send for my momma and my sister.

INJUN BILL
You about as far from makin' your way as one man can get.

FROGGY
Do not mistake my current... sloppiness... for being a bum. I ain't a bum.

(INJUN BILL starts packing up)

FROGGY
Look. When I got kicked out of the army, I... fell on hard times. I'm a big enough man to admit it.

INJUN BILL
Yes you are.

FROGGY
And so I... hey! Was you callin' me fat again?

INJUN BILL
Just go on.

FROGGY
No! I wanna know if you was...

INJUN BILL
GO ON!

FROGGY
So alls I need is some direction. I'm a hell of a cook. Best you ever seen. I'm gonna head to Billings, and set me up a restaurant. Then, I send for my kin. Ain't seen 'em in ten years. *(He pulls a photo out of his pocket)* See there? That's my momma. And that little darlin' is my sister Annabelle. Well, ain't so little now, I guess. Be eighteen if I got my numbers right.

(INJUN BILL starts to leave)

FROGGY
Where you goin'?

INJUN BILL
I gotta see a man about some shoes.

FROGGY
Right. But where's that?

INJUN BILL
It don't matter.

FROGGY
If it don't matter, then tell me.

INJUN BILL
Fuck off, fat man! I don't gotta tell you nothin'!

FROGGY
Oh! I'm sorry! I figured what with me bein' responsible for bustin' you outta jail, you might treat me with certain... hospitalitude!

(Beat)

INJUN BILL
Goddammit. I'm going to Billings.

FROGGY
Billings? Billings, Montana?

INJUN BILL
Yeah.

FROGGY
Smack my ass! That's where I'm goin'.

INJUN BILL
I caught that.

FROGGY
Let me go with you.

INJUN BILL
No.

FROGGY
Please?

INJUN BILL
You just slow me down.

FROGGY
I won't bother you. Hand to god.

INJUN BILL
No.

FROGGY
I'll cook for you! Gimme the right spices, and I can make a buzzard taste like sirloin steak.

INJUN BILL
No.

FROGGY
I'll play my harmonica.

(That makes INJUN BILL stop)

FROGGY
Yessir. Whenever you want. I know lots of songs, too. Clementine and Dog Spit Blues and...

INJUN BILL
You know Let the Circle Be Unbroken?

FROGGY
Yes. Yes I do.

INJUN BILL
I like that one. Makes me feel...something.

FROGGY
So I can come with ya?

INJUN BILL
'Til I get sick of ya.

FROGGY
(shaking BILL's hand roughly) Thank you, Mr. Injun Bill. You will not regret it.

INJUN BILL
I gotta make one thing clear. We ain't friends. You get me?

FROGGY
I get you.

INJUN BILL
You can follow me. You can play the mouth harp. But we ain't friends.

FROGGY
I can live with that.

INJUN BILL
All right then.

(FROGGY looks at INJUN BILL)

FROGGY
Wait. You forgot your... I'll get it.

(FROGGY goes through the supplies)

FROGGY
Where the hell's your gun?

INJUN BILL
I ain't got one.

FROGGY
You ain't got a gun?

INJUN BILL
No.

FROGGY
What the hell kind of outlaw gots no gun?

INJUN BILL
I don't use guns. Not anymore.

FROGGY
What? Guns are great! They take all the diffi... difcult... trouble out of killin' a man.

INJUN BILL
That's why I don't like 'em. You kill a man with a gun... don't take no more skill than pointing a finger. But a knife...

(INJUN BILL closes on FROGGY)

INJUN BILL
With a knife, you gotta get in close. You gotta know how to fight, gotta be quick. That's how a man fights. How a man kills. You get me?

FROGGY
I feel I gotta be honest with you. I'm one scary sentence away from pissing myself. I bring this up on account of I got no other pants.

(Beat. INJUN BILL slaps FROGGY on the shoulder and laughs)

INJUN BILL
Come on. We're killin' daylight.

FROGGY
Where we goin'?

INJUN BILL
Like any good sinner, we're headin' South.

(INJUN BILL leaves. FROGGY quickly checks the front of his pants)

FROGGY
Goddamn, that was a close one.

(He runs after INJUN BILL. Lights change)

Scene 3

ACTOR 1
(singing)
So Bill headed to Montana
With a partner that plain galled him
Froggy was the name they called him
When they got the chance to speak
But the city that they came to
Looked like God had set a flame to
None left there but cold dead corpses
'Round a chapel, burned and bleak

(An abandoned church in Northern Montana. Night. The place looks ransacked. FROGGY pokes his head through the door. He has a broken chair leg for a club. He looks around, leaping between pews. Satisfied, he goes back to the door)

FROGGY
What the hell happened to this town?

INJUN BILL
Goddamn blood bath.

FROGGY
I ain't seen so many dead folks since Little Bighorn. *(He stops, stares at INJUN BILL)* Now remember – y'all won that one.

INJUN BILL
Grab that pew. We're gonna put it against the door.

FROGGY
How come?

INJUN BILL
If whoever killed this town is out there, I don't want him gettin' in here.

FROGGY
That is solid thinking.

(They grab the pew and move it to the door. FROGGY plops down on a different pew while INJUN BILL searches the room)

INJUN BILL
We shouldn't have stopped here.

FROGGY
Bill, we been on the road all day and damn near all night. When my sweaty balls stick to my leg for too long, I get irritable.

INJUN BILL
We shoulda camped outside of town.

FROGGY
Look. I didn't know this place had gone tits up when we got here, all right? I figured we'd hit the saloon, stake out a couple of rooms...

INJUN BILL
...whole place feels wrong...

FROGGY
...hook up a card game, maybe do a little alley-catin'...

(INJUN BILL stares at him)

FROGGY
I got needs, Bill. And I'm saying this for your benefit; you look like you could use a good... *(FROGGY's gesture indicates a blowjob)* That comes from a place of kindness.

(INJUN BILL sits, takes a whetstone to a knife)

FROGGY
Well, I'm out. See ya in the morning.

(FROGGY lies down, attempting to sleep. The sound of the whetstone makes it impossible. He tosses and turns, finally just stares at INJUN BILL. INJUN BILL speaks without even looking back)

INJUN BILL
Different knives got different functions. My big Bowie... that's if you wanna end it quick. They call it a knife, but it's damn near a sword. Now this sweet girl... *(Holds up the one he's sharpening)* I call her Quiet Annie. I keep her sharp as a scalpel. Small as she is, you can slide her right in and a fella won't even feel it. Not if you put her in the Sweet Spot. Might even pass out before he even sees the blood.

FROGGY
Bill. I can respect a man who's passionate about his work. But that little speech don't help my restfulness at all.

(INJUN BILL stares at him, confused)

INJUN BILL
I say somethin'?

FROGGY
Hell yes! You just told me the fuckin' life and times of Quiet Annie!

INJUN BILL
No I didn't.

FROGGY
Then why am I scared for my life right this second? And how did I know her name?

INJUN BILL
I was just thinkin' 'bout her is all.

FROGGY
Well, then you were thinking real goddamn loud, 'cause I heard it all the way over here.

(INJUN BILL sits, confused)

INJUN BILL
Huh.

FROGGY
You talk to yourself. That's all.

INJUN BILL
I do?

FROGGY
Yeah. I'm guessin' you ain't had company for a while, so you don't notice it.

INJUN BILL
Huh.

FROGGY
And if I might hazard another word of advice... you need to talk more.

INJUN BILL
Hmm.

FROGGY
I'm basin' this on that completely mortifyin' bedtime story you just told me.

INJUN BILL
I like knives.

FROGGY
Fair enough. But can you see how maybe it's not somethin' I want to hear about as I sleep in the abandoned church of a town full of dead folk?

(INJUN BILL puts his knife away)

INJUN BILL
I don't like talkin'.

FROGGY
All's I'm sayin' is we all need a friendly ear sometimes.

(INJUN BILL stares at him)

FROGGY
Right, right. We ain't friends. But I'm close as you got now.

(INJUN BILL gets up, wanders as he speaks)

INJUN BILL
I had a friend once. George Parrot. Ever heard of him?

FROGGY
Yeah, yeah. But they called him something else...

INJUN BILL
Big Nose George.

FROGGY
That's it.

INJUN BILL
Only friend I ever had. He's dead now.

FROGGY
Sorry to hear that.

INJUN BILL
Bein' only a half-breed... I never fit in nowhere. The Lakotas hated me. My pa's people hated me. But George liked me. Said I was funny.

FROGGY
Yeah, you're a real gut-buster. *(Beat)* Go on.

INJUN BILL
I joined up with him when I was 14. Stealin' cattle mostly. Robbin' coaches and banks, too. George was the one who taught me how to kill. He saw how much hate I had inside me and said "Billy-boy"... he called me "Billy Boy"...

FROGGY
All right.

INJUN BILL
He said "Hate's a good thing. Makes the world go 'round, and murder keeps it interesting."

FROGGY
Jesus Christ.

INJUN BILL
Pretty smart, huh?

FROGGY
That ain't smart! It's batshit crazy!

(INJUN BILL glares at him)

FROGGY
You know what? I was speakin' in haste.

INJUN BILL
What do you know about it? Only thing you ever killed was peace and quiet!

FROGGY
How's that?

INJUN BILL
I gotta wonder.... did your ass get big 'cause it was jealous of how big your mouth was?

FROGGY
You sayin' I'm fat?!

INJUN BILL
Yes! Yes, goddammit! That is exactly what I'm sayin!!!

(Beat. Instead of anger, FROGGY is genuinely hurt)

FROGGY
I know about killin', Bill. Custer told me all about it.

INJUN BILL
I don't care.

FROGGY
He said "Son, you kill for two reasons only: If

your life is in danger, or if the life of someone you care about's in danger. Those are the kills Jesus doesn't give two shits about."

(They sit in uncomfortable silence for a bit)

FROGGY
What happened to him? Big Nose George, I mean.

(INJUN BILL falls silent)

FROGGY
Just... 'cause you said he was dead, and I figured...

(INJUN BILL bursts into action, shouting & knocking things over. After a bit, he hangs his head in despair)

INJUN BILL
He's shoes, Froggy.

(Beat)

FROGGY
What?

INJUN BILL
Two years back, they caught George and the rest of the gang back in Wyoming. Twenty-thousand dollar bounty on his head.

FROGGY
Damn.

INJUN BILL
Before he even got his trial, lynch mob got him. Strung him up on a goddamn telegraph pole. If it had ended there... shit, that would've been bad enough but... *(He stops to collect himself)* Some rich asshole doctor bought George's body.

FROGGY
Oh lord...

INJUN BILL
Cut up his skull. Said he wanted to study his brain. But then why'd he skin his chest, huh? Why'd he skin his legs?

FROGGY
I don't...

INJUN BILL
So he could make ruttin' shoes out of my dead friend George! That's why!

(Beat)

FROGGY
I feel like maybe you ain't got your facts right.

INJUN BILL
Oh, I ain't done.

FROGGY
That's fine, but...

INJUN BILL
That self-same bastard...he's governor of Wyoming now. A corpse-cuttin' son of a bitch, and he's a governor! And... AND... he wore them shoes to his inauguration! Walkin' 'round, shakin' hands and kissin' babies... with my dead friend on his feet!

FROGGY
Just calm down there...

INJUN BILL
John Eugene Osborne! That's the bastard's name, and I curse it to Hell! Damn you, John Osborne!

And damn your god-forsaken footwear!

(Beat)

FROGGY
Now I want you to know right off that I'm not callin' you a liar...

INJUN BILL
You don't believe me?!

FROGGY
Men don't make other men into shoes.

INJUN BILL
I was like you once. Naïve.

FROGGY
Lord...

INJUN BILL
I gotta hunt down the shoes, Froggy. I gotta hunt them down, and kill the no-good, stinkin', ruttin' bastard is wearin' 'em.

(Beat)

FROGGY
See? Don't that feel better?

INJUN BILL
You don't know. I've been hunting Osborne for 2 damn years...it takes its toll. Ain't easy getting' to a Governor. I gotta get him this time. I gotta. This time, either he ends up dead or I do.

FROGGY
You want I should find a confessional?

(INJUN BILL stares at him, almost amused)

FROGGY
What?

INJUN BILL
I only ever told that story once before. To a priest.

FROGGY
You don't strike me as the church-going type.

INJUN BILL
Poor bastard was in the cell next to me, year or two back.

FROGGY
They put priests in jail now?

INJUN BILL
Ain't thought about him in a long time. Must be all this... churchiness.

FROGGY
I don't know. I like church folk. Always got a... calmness to 'em, you know?

(Suddenly, a figure lurches out of the dark. It is a nun, her clothes stained and her demeanor crazed)

SISTER BERNADETTE
And when he had opened the fourth seal...!

FROGGY/INJUN BILL
AAAAAH!

SISTER BERNADETTE
...I heard the voice of the fourth beast say... Come and see! *(She staggers to* FROGGY, *grabbing him by the shoulders)* Come and see!

FROGGY
Get this crazy bitch off me!

SISTER BERNADETTE
COME AND SEE!

(INJUN BILL pulls his sword, as SISTER BERNADETTE staggers to the pulpit)

SISTER BERNADETTE
And I looked, and BEHOLD! A pale horse! And his name that sat on him was Death, and Hell followed with him!

(She slams her head on the pulpit, perhaps having passed out. FROGGY & INJUN BILL just stare at each other for a bit)

FROGGY
Bill?

INJUN BILL
Yeah?

FROGGY
I'm feelin' a mite unnerved right now.

INJUN BILL
Yeah.

(SISTER BERNADETTE quickly raises her head, launching back into her sermon. FROGGY & INJUN BILL leap in surprise)

SISTER BERNADETTE
Death has come to Garden Ridge, sisters! And he has left naught but damnation is his wake!

(BILL & FROGGY bolt for the door. In attempting to remove the pew, they get in each other's way and achieve nothing)

SISTER BERNADETTE
Prepare to render your souls unto God our

deliverer! None shall be spared, for this is the hour of his righteous judgment! *(She points at people who aren't there)* Guilty! *(She points again)* Guilty! *(She points at FROGGY & BILL, her eyes growing wide, her voice deadly serious)* Guilty!

FROGGY
Ma'am, that's the sort of behavior what keeps people from going to Church.

(She staggers towards them. They redouble their efforts to get out, but fail)

SISTER BERNADETTE
You must flee this place!

INJUN BILL
We're tryin'!

SISTER BERNADETTE
The pale horseman has ridden through our city, and taken the lives of all!

FROGGY
Well, obviously not all…

SISTER BERNADETTE
He killed the father! He killed the Mother Superior! Only Bernadette was spared, that she may proclaim his coming to the world!

INJUN BILL
Good for you.

SISTER BERNADETTE
And the stars of Heaven fell unto the Earth, even as a fig tree ceaseth her untimely figs when she is shaken of a mighty wind!

FROGGY
Untimely figs?

SISTER BERNADETTE
And they cried with a loud voice, saying "O Lord, holy and true, dost thou not judge me and avenge our blood on them that dwell on Earth?!"

(INJUN BILL gives up on the door, grabbing SISTER BERNADETTE)

INJUN BILL
Ma'am! I need you to come to your goddamn senses!

SISTER BERNADETTE
(Grabbing INJUN BILL by the ear) This is still a church, young lady.

INJUN BILL
Sister, I would take it kindly if you would just tell me what the fuck happened here?

FROGGY
Or we could just leave. Yep. Let's do that.

SISTER BERNADETTE
Judgment Day, sisters! Revelation is upon us.

INJUN BILL
A man done this killing, didn't he?

SISTER BERNADETTE
Yes.

INJUN BILL
A man on a horse?

SISTER BERNADETTE
The pale horseman. And Hell followed with him.

(She staggers about, attempting to remember the events)

SISTER BERNADETTE
He appeared as a mortal man...rode into the square on a horse white as bleached bones... questions he had...answers he demanded...He spoke to Father Gregory...so much anger...he looked at all of us...looked into us, into our very souls, and judged us sinners all. Then with gun and sword, he cut us down. He left only me alive. I clutched his boot and cried out "What is your name? You who are the fire and fury of God... what is your name?"

FROGGY
What...what did he say?

SISTER BERNADETTE
"Death". He said his name... was Death.

(They stand there, terrified. FROGGY sees a collection plate. He picks it up, drops some coins in it)

FROGGY
The service has ended. May you go in peace to love and to serve the lord.

(He hurls the pew out of the way, opens the door and bolts. INJUN BILL follows. SISTER BERNADETTE sits on a pew)

SISTER BERNADETTE
Death has come for us all.

(Lights fade)

Scene 4

ACTOR 2
(singing)
INJUN BILL, INJUN BILL
FLEE THE CHURCH BEFORE HE FINDS YOU
'CAUSE DEATH FOLLOWS RIGHT BEHIND YOU
AND YOUR JOURNEY'S FAR FROM DONE
INJUN BILL, INJUN BILL
RIDE TO BILLINGS AND TO GLORY
WELL, THIS AIN'T THAT KIND OF STORY
SO JUST WATCH THE SETTING SUN

(Billings, Montana. The next day. A large outdoor bathtub is onstage. INJUN BILL sits at the foot of it. FROGGY lifts head out of the water, sopping wet)

FROGGY
Goddamn! That is what the doctor ordered!

(He shakes his head vigorously, soaking INJUN BILL)

INJUN BILL
Watch it!

FROGGY
Bill, you gotta get in one of these! Wash the stink right off ya.

INJUN BILL
I don't stink.

FROGGY
Well I did! And now I feel like a new man. Don't know what your business is in Billings, but hallelujah! Here we are!

INJUN BILL
Gotta talk to a man at the saloon.

FROGGY
WOO! Got my clothes warshed, got my body warshed. Next I'm gonna buy me some smell'um for my hair, some wax for my whiskers, and get me some tail.

INJUN BILL
You get yourself cleaned up, then you're gonna go balls-deep in some stinking whore?

FROGGY
No sir! I'm gonna get me the best…

(He reaches over, grabbing his wallet)

FROGGY
The best thirteen dollar-and-82-cent whore money can buy.

INJUN BILL
Where you get all that money?

(Beat. FROGGY has been caught, and can't think of a good lie to get out of it)

FROGGY
Distant relation?

(INJUN BILL grabs him and shoves his head under the water. FROGGY struggles, and BILL lets him up)

FROGGY
Jesus Christ!

INJUN BILL
You lie to me again, I'm holdin' you down there for ten minutes!

FROGGY
I took it off the dead folks! You happy now, you crazy som'bitch!?

INJUN BILL
You what?

FROGGY
Them dead folk in Garden Ridge! While you was inspecting the town, I was makin' donations to the Get-Froggy-Bathed-And-Humped fund.

INJUN BILL
That's low, Froggy. Stealin' from dead folks is low.

FROGGY
I don't need no moral condemnation from some half-Injun foot-cutter.

INJUN BILL
I'm on a quest for vengeance. I'm doin' what I gotta do. And I ain't gotta steal from dead folk.

FROGGY
...just mad that you didn't think of it first...

INJUN BILL
Now here's an interesting thought to throw at ya. What kind of man kills a whole damn town, but don't take their money?

FROGGY
That is an interesting thought. A rich man?

INJUN BILL
I never met a rich man wouldn't stop a train if he saw a nickel on the tracks.

FROGGY
Fair enough. So I guess you gotta ask yourself... what kind of man don't care about money?

INJUN BILL
A dangerous man.

FROGGY
Yes. Thank you for that, Bill. The fact that he killed fifty people didn't clue me in to his dangerous nature.

(MADAME FLORA enters. She is a large, heavily coifed & made-up woman)

MADAME FLORA
Howdy, boys. You new to these parts?

FROGGY
That we are, ma'am.

MADAME FLORA
Madame, sugar. Madame Flora, at yer service.

FROGGY
Hot damn. I think you might be just what I'm

lookin' for.

(She leans in close, hand in the water)

MADAME FLORA
Is that a fact?

(FROGGY jumps)

FROGGY
I... that is to say... you run the local brothel?

MADAME FLORA
I cater to the needs of the menfolk, introducing them to ladies of my acquaintance for a small fee.

FROGGY
Madame Flora, I am in dire need of feminine companionship this night.

MADAME FLORA
Sugar, you came to the right town.

(INJUN BILL rises, going to leave)

MADAME FLORA
My my my my my. Who is this tall drink of handsome?

FROGGY
That's my friend Bill. Bill, say howdy to the lady.

(INJUN BILL tips his hat)

INJUN BILL
Miss. And we ain't friends.

(MADAME FLORA moves in on BILL)

MADAME FLORA
I am duty-bound to ask if you are also in need

of companionship. And if you absolutely have to know, I'm very much hopin' that I'm just your type.

INJUN BILL
You ain't.

(She slaps BILL)

INJUN BILL
That is to say… I don't roll with trade that speaks English.

MADAME FLORA
I see. While I'm disappointed that I won't be riding you into the sunset, I can respect a man who knows what he wants and doesn't mince words about it.

INJUN BILL
That's fine, but I ain't lookin' to roll.

FROGGY
Madame Flora, he don't speak for the both of us.

MADAME FLORA
Not even for Bjarma?

(BILL stops. The name is pronounced BYAR-ma)

INJUN BILL
What kind of name is Bjarma?

MADAME FLORA
Faroese, and that's a fact.

INJUN BILL
Where she from?

MADAME FLORA
The Faroe Islands.

INJUN BILL
Where's that?

MADAME FLORA
Up north, by Denmark. Little island chain, not much on it but sheep and buxom ladies. And William... she doesn't speak a word of English. Not. One. Syllable.

FROGGY
Come on, Bill. That's gotta be some kind of sign.

(Beat)

INJUN BILL
How much?

MADAME FLORA
Specialty acts like Bjarma cost ten up front.

(BILL hands her a ten dollar bill)

FROGGY
Where you get that money?

INJUN BILL
Had a stash in the cave.

FROGGY
How much for a regular-speakin' whore, Miss?

MADAME FLORA
In the front, or 'round back?

FROGGY
In the front.

MADAME FLORA
Five dollars.

FROGGY
Sold!

(FROGGY starts to rise, with BILL grabbing a towel to cover him at the last second)

MADAME FLORA
I appreciate the gallantry, sir. But I'm sure this gentleman doesn't have anything I haven't seen...

(She looks on the other side of the curtain, surprised by what she sees)

MADAME FLORA
Oh my.

(FROGGY smiles proudly)

FROGGY
And that's why I wear my pants loose.

(Lights fade)

Scene 5

(The brothel, moments later. BELLE, a beautiful young prostitute sits on a bed. FROGGY enters. He is noticeably cleaner, with his hair and moustache styled)

FROGGY
Oh my lord. Ain't you as sweet as cinnamon.

BELLE
Am I?

FROGGY
You are indeed. You are indeed.

(She offers her hand)

BELLE
I'm Belle.

FROGGY
They call me Froggy.

(He kisses her hand)

BELLE
Well. Most men shake my hand. Those who don't throw me to the bed, that is. You know your manners.

FROGGY
My mama raised me right.

BELLE
Clearly.

(She pats the bed. He joins her. She rubs his shoulders. He moans in pleasure)

FROGGY
Miss Belle, before tonight, I believed myself to be just about the unluckiest som'bitch walkin' the earth. I admit I may have been wrong on that subject.

BELLE
Am I your rabbit's foot then? *(She puts her foot on his lap)*

FROGGY
You just might be.

(He moves in to kiss her. She moves him to her neck)

BELLE
Not on the lips, dear. Never the lips.

FROGGY
Yes, ma'am. I was wonderin' if I could ask a favor of you.

BELLE
It's your dollar, darlin'.

FROGGY
Could you...just stand right there? *(He moves her in front of a lamp, so she is now silhouetted by the light)* That's it. Perfect. Now, could you undress for me?

BELLE
That is usually the preferred way to go.

FROGGY
I mean... slow. Undress slow.

BELLE
Your wish is my command. *(She slowly removes her clothing)* I like you, Froggy.

FROGGY
You do?

BELLE
Most men who come through these parts... they just throw my skirts up over my shoulders and get to it. I like a man who can enjoy the female form.

FROGGY
Oh. I'm enjoying it.

(She has removed her vest, and begins undoing her corset)

FROGGY
Slower.

BELLE
All right then. *(She slowly works on her corset)*

BELLE
You a soldier, Froggy? I'm guessing you are on account of your pants and your hat.

FROGGY
I was, ma'am. Dishonorably discharged on account of drunkenness, horse-thievery and general ineptitude.

BELLE
You don't seem drunk now.

FROGGY
That's what I'm doin' after.

BELLE
And you certainly don't seem inept.

FROGGY
That's kind of you to say, but I'll tell you the truth.

BELLE
Please do.

FROGGY
Only thing I was ever good at was cookin'. That's why I come out this way.

BELLE
To be a cook?

FROGGY
Yes, ma'am. I mean to open a restaurant. I hear tell Billings done sprung up good, what with the new train runnin' through it. I figure, trains bring more people, and them people gotta eat.

BELLE
Aren't you enterprising?

FROGGY
My mama always told me "Be a cook or be an undertaker. People always gotta eat, and they

always gotta die."

BELLE
So why not an undertaker?

FROGGY
Well, dead folks got an odor to 'em.

BELLE
I see. Well Froggy, do you have a specialty?

FROGGY
Um... well... I'm good South of the border, if you get my meaning...

(BELLE laughs, removing her corset)

BELLE
I mean with your cooking.

FROGGY
Oh! Right, I... You know what I really want to do is start up a Cajun restaurant somewhere 'round here.

BELLE
Really?

FROGGY
Oh yeah. I'm from Louisiana. Nothing better than that smell when you're lettin' the roux brown up, throwin' in some sassafras and some andouille...

BELLE
I'm from Louisiana myself.

FROGGY
No!

BELLE
God's honest truth. Left when I was just a girl.

FROGGY
Where abouts?

BELLE
Baton Rouge.

FROGGY
No kiddin'? I'm from Baton Rouge! Slower.

(BELLE slowly removes her stockings)

FROGGY
You don't have an accent.

BELLE
Worked hard to lose it. Some folks think it makes you sound ignorant.

FROGGY
Fellas in the army said the same thing. Turns out I sound ignorant with or without it.

(She laughs at that)

FROGGY
Goddamn! A fine lookin' Louisiana gal just like my momma would want me to marry.

BELLE
Oh hush.

FROGGY
You know Old Man Montpellier? Mixed fella that runs the bakery on Convention Street?

BELLE
Know him? Hell, we were practically neighbors!

FROGGY
I used to steal croissants from his window every morning when he was in the back! Well, me and

the fellas I ran with.

BELLE
No!

FROGGY
I did!

BELLE
You must've known my brother then! I bet he was one of your gang!

FROGGY
Wouldn't that be just too much?

BELLE
You know Jean-Phillipe Baptiste?

(Long, awkward beat)

FROGGY
What?

BELLE
That was my brother's name. Sandy blonde hair, thin as a rail.

FROGGY
Oh sweet Jesus.

BELLE
He left... must've been ten years ago. Got killed fighting with General Custer. *(She sees the look of utter horror on his face)* Do you know him, Froggy?

(FROGGY says nothing, his expression frozen)

BELLE
Froggy?

FROGGY
Annabelle?

(Beat)

BELLE
Did Flora tell you my Christian name?

FROGGY
Annabelle, it's me!

BELLE
Me who?

FROGGY
Jean-Fucking-Philippe!

(Beat)

BELLE
That's not nice.

FROGGY
I know, but it's the goddamn truth!

(BELLE goes to him, places her hand on his face. She pushes his cheeks back, trying to picture him thinner. She sees it)

BELLE
Jean-Philippe?

FROGGY
Uh-huh.

(BELLE hugs him. FROGGY hesitantly hugs her back)

BELLE
Oh my god! You're alive! They told us you took two arrows to the face!

FROGGY
I imagine they was tryin' to be kind.

BELLE
Why didn't you come back to us?

FROGGY
I was ashamed. I wanted to hold to my word, build my restaurant.

BELLE
But ten years?! Seven of which I thought you were dead!

FROGGY
What about Mama? You gotta tell her...

BELLE
Jean-Philippe, Mama passed.

(He lowers his head, crushed)

FROGGY
...no...

BELLE
She got the TB in her lungs. It was quicker for her than it was for most. When she heard that Jesus had called you home... I think she just wanted to go.

(FROGGY sits on the bed, defeated)

BELLE
I'm so sorry. If I knew you were still with us, I'd have tracked you down.

FROGGY
I shoulda gone home. Instead, I shoved my head in a bottle and never come out.

BELLE
We still have each other. You're not alone. *(She touches his arm gently)*

FROGGY
I can't believe she's gone, Anna. All this time, I been holdin' on to this belief that... and lookit what I am now! A fat drunk in a whorehouse! Maybe that's what I should call my restaurant!

(He laughs at that. She does as well)

BELLE
And what about me? I've been rolling with johns for the better part of a year. I think things went just ducky for the both of us!

(They laugh again)

FROGGY
I know! I was about to be one of those johns!

(They laugh again, then stare at each other. She goes to the window and vomits just as he grabs an empty chamber pot and vomits)

FROGGY
OH GOD! OH MY GOD! What have I done!?

BELLE
(Scrambling to dress herself) Unclean! I'm unclean!

FROGGY
Anna, I... I gotta go!

BELLE
I'm a monster!

FROGGY
I'll... visit or... something I... so long.

(He heads for the door, muttering as he goes)

FROGGY
...unluckiest som'bitch walkin' the earth...

(Lights fade)

Scene 6

(The brothel, but a different room, at the same time as Scene 5. INJUN BILL paces, waiting for BJARMA. He finds a tall mirror & inspects himself in it. He fiddles with his knives, then realizes he should remove his knife belt. He does so as BJARMA enters)

MADAME FLORA
Last chance to change your mind. *(Beat)* It could've been... magic. *(She exits)*

INJUN BILL
You're beautiful.

(She curtsies)

INJUN BILL
Do you... beautiful. Do you know that word?

(She smiles at him)

INJUN BILL
Beautiful? You are... forget it.

(She sits on the bed, motioning for him to join her)

BJARMA
Bola? (Sit?)

INJUN BILL
Is that... you want me to sit?

(He sits next to her. They share a moment of uncertainty. She then puts her hand high on his leg)

INJUN BILL
No. That's all right.

(She stares at him, confused. She then raises her arms in the air, wrists together, inquiring if he wants to tie her up)

INJUN BILL
No. No, nothing like that.

BJARMA
Als kyn? (No sex?)

INJUN BILL
You don't know what I'm saying, do you? No English?

BJARMA
Foroyskt. Als Enskt. (Faroese. No English)

INJUN BILL
Goddamn, you got a pretty way of talking. I'm... my name is Bill. *(He points to himself)* Bill.

BJARMA
Beel.

INJUN BILL
Now say your name.

BJARMA
Beel?

INJUN BILL
No. I'm Bill. You are...?

BJARMA
Bjarma.

INJUN BILL
That's real pretty. Like you.

(They smile at each other, not talking)

BJARMA
Nuh i hafa kyn? (Now we have sex?)

INJUN BILL
(Taking her hands in his) Darlin', I know I might as well be speaking Chinee to ya, but I'm hoping you'll pick up my meaning none the less. It would mean an awful lot to me if I could just... here.

(He leans her back on the bed. She's confused but lets him)

INJUN BILL
And I'm gonna...

(He leans back against her, his head resting on her chest. She instinctively puts her arms around him)

INJUN BILL
That's it. Yes. That's exactly what I want. I just want to lie here like this.

(She strokes his hair)

INJUN BILL
Thank you.

(They lie there in silence for a bit)

INJUN BILL
I never knew my father. He was a cavalryman, stuck it to my mama and left. She had to leave her people, 'cause of the shame. She hated me. My whole life, she looked at me with nothin' but a wish that I was dead. One day, she just up and left. I was ten. Hell, I don't know why it took her so long to do it. Bjarma…

(She looks at him)

INJUN BILL
Used to be I'd hump a girl, pull up my pants and walk out the door. The first time a woman just…held me after… I cried. Cried like a damn baby. So if I end up doin' that again, I'm hopin' you'll be sympathetic to my situation. *(Beat)* Damn near all my life, I been hated. And the only folks that didn't hate me are dead now. Them bastards that caught George, they was after the bounty. Twenty-thousand dollars 'cause George shot a deputy in the face. 'Cept it wasn't George that shot the man. He told folks he did, 'cause he liked to brag. That was always his way. But George… he could shove a gun up a man's ass and he'd still miss. *(Beat)* They killed George 'cause of what I done. What I done, and what I let him say he did. 'Cause I thought it would make him happy. And now… I'm wantin' to make amends, but in my heart… I don't know why the hell I'm doing this. I'm doin' what George would've done…but is that a reason to do somethin'? The man's dead two years now, and he's still tellin' me what to do. I feel like I

owe it to him, but all he ever give me was this... wreck of a life. Is that somethin' to be grateful for?

(He stares at her. She stares back, confused. She puts her mouth around his nose. Beat)

INJUN BILL
I don't know if this is stimulatin' where you come from, but it's doin' nothin' for me.

(Suddenly, a loud knock on the door)

FROGGY
(offstage) Injun Bill? We're goin'. Now!

INJUN BILL
Gimme a minute here.

FROGGY
(offstage) Now!

(BILL rises, grabs his belt, and kisses BJARMA sweetly)

INJUN BILL
Thanks for listenin', Bjarma. You're a peach.

(He leaves. BJARMA lies back in bed, holding her head)

BJARMA
Jesus Christ. Why do I always get the crazy ones?

(Lights fade)

Scene 7

ACTOR 1
(singing)
AT A TAVERN NAME OF CROSSROADS,
BILL & FROGGY CAME A CALLIN'
FOR A BARKEEP SO APPALLIN'
HE HAD HELLFIRE ON THE TAP
BUT THE MAN OF WHOM I'M SPEAKIN'
HAD THE KNOWLEDGE THEY WERE SEEKIN'
SO BILL NEVER STOPPED TO WONDER
IF THE MEETING WAS A TRAP

(Crossroads Saloon, later that night. The sound of a crowd talking, and old time piano music. ABEL WEXFORD is cleaning the bar. He's a rough looking Irishman w/ an eye patch. INJUN BILL & FROGGY enter. FROGGY already has a bottle & is fairly drunk. INJUN BILL smiles widely, throws his hands in the air and shouts his friend's name)

INJUN BILL
Abel Wexford!

(ABEL smiles wide, throws his hands up and responds in kind)

ABEL
Injun Bill Picote!

(Without changing his expression, he pulls a gun from beneath the bar and fires. INJUN BILL & FROGGY duck for cover. The crowd grows silent, and the music stops)

FROGGY
Jesus Christ!

INJUN BILL
Just calm down, Abel!

ABEL
How can I be calm when one of me favorite people just walked through me door? *(He fires again)* Come on over! Let me give ya a hug!

(He fires again, but the gun jams. INJUN BILL quickly runs over & wrestles the gun from him)

ABEL
Still pretty quick, are ya?

INJUN BILL
Quick enough.

ABEL
Think so? *(He pulls a derringer out of his jacket. INJUN BILL grabs it)*

ABEL
Damn!

FROGGY
Can I stand up now?

(ABEL *hurls himself at* INJUN BILL. *They fall to the ground wrestling. As they do,* FROGGY *heads over to the bar and starts pouring himself drinks*)

FROGGY
Get 'em, Bill.

(INJUN BILL *ends up on top of* ABEL, *his Bowie knife to* ABEL's *throat*)

INJUN BILL
You gonna settle down now, Abel?

ABEL
I'm half-deaf, Bill! I can't hear you!

INJUN BILL
I said...

(INJUN BILL *leans in and* ABEL *head-butts him.* INJUN BILL *staggers back*)

ABEL
I'm truly surprised you fell fer that.

(ABEL *almost charges again, but* FROGGY *grabs him, putting him in a full-nelson*)

FROGGY
That's enough, barkeep.

ABEL
Let me go!

FROGGY
Not a Chinaman's chance!

ABEL
I mean ta kill that redskin shitbird!

FROGGY
And that's why I'm not lettin' you go.

(INJUN BILL rises, crosses to them)

INJUN BILL
You still pissed off about the eye?

ABEL
No, it's a distant feckin' memory. What eye are you speakin' of?

INJUN BILL
It was an accident and you know it.

ABEL
Oh thank god! Now I can see outta my left side again.

INJUN BILL
Abel, I come here for answers. Once I get 'em, I'll leave. *(Slams some bills on the table)*

ABEL
What's that?

INJUN BILL
My appreciation for the answers.

ABEL
How much?

(FROGGY & ABEL hobble over to the table. ABEL counts the bills)

ABEL
Why don't I pour you fellas some drinks?

(FROGGY lets ABEL go)

ABEL
Name your firewater, redskin.

INJUN BILL
Bourbon if you got it.

ABEL
I do. What about you, tiny?

FROGGY
Gimme somethin' that'll knock me on my ass. I got some forgettin' to do.

ABEL
Comin' up. Franky! Get back ta that piana or I'll box yer ears for ya!

(The crowd starts talking again, and the music starts back up. He slides them their drinks. FROGGY downs his, then goes down to one knee)

FROGGY
Good god.

ABEL
That's straight from the homeland, boyo. Now, onto our business.

INJUN BILL
You know where they are?

ABEL
What "they" would that be?

INJUN BILL
Don't bust my balls, Abel. That letter you sent said you knew.

ABEL
Ever think I sent that to get you here so I could put a bullet in yer brain?

(INJUN BILL draws a knife)

INJUN BILL
That best be a lie. Otherwise, Quiet Annie might have to enter negotiations.

ABEL
All right, all right, all right. Jesus.

(As they talk, FROGGY rises, signals for another drink. ABEL pours him another)

ABEL
The Governor is headin' down to Denver this very week. Might already be there.

INJUN BILL
Why Denver?

ABEL
They say he's investin' in a gold mine. S'posed to be real hush-hush, so I figure he won't have his full entourage, if you get my meaning.

FROGGY
...can't believe I nearly ram-rodded my own sister...

(ABEL & INJUN BILL stare at him)

FROGGY
What? I didn't... nothin'.

INJUN BILL
How do I know he'll have the shoes?

ABEL
Way I hear tell, he don't go nowhere without 'em. It's a point of pride.

INJUN BILL
Pride is a deadly sin.

ABEL
Yes it is.

INJUN BILL
Reckon it's high-time he finds out how deadly. Come on, Froggy.

(He grabs FROGGY, mutters to himself)

INJUN BILL
I'm comin' for you, Osborne. You ain't slippin' away this time, you son of a whore.

ABEL
Hey! Come back here and I'll kill ya. You hear me? Don't let me see you again.

INJUN BILL
Then I guess I'll just stay to your left.

(He and FROGGY head out. Lights fade)

Scene 8

ACTOR 2
(singing)
Injun Bill, Injun Bill
Think on this before you slaughter
Every girl is someone's daughter,
Every man is someone's son
Injun Bill, Injun Bill
Let your better Angels guide you
'Cause the Devil that's inside you
Wants his due before it's done

(Later. A train station. FROGGY's alone. INJUN BILL soon walks up, carrying a package)

FROGGY
What'cha got there?

INJUN BILL
Trail rations. It's 500 miles to Denver, and I reckon I gotta eat sometime in there.

FROGGY
Where's mine?

(Beat)

INJUN BILL
Where's your what?

FROGGY
Where's my food?

INJUN BILL
I think Abel's saloon has potatoes or some such.

FROGGY
I mean, my rations. I gotta eat too.

INJUN BILL
What the hell are you talkin' about? You're stayin' here.

FROGGY
Nope.

INJUN BILL
This was where you were going. Billings. Well, look around! You're here. I'm headin' out tonight, so don't get mushy on me.

FROGGY
I'm comin' with you.

INJUN BILL
The hell you say.

FROGGY
The hell I do say!

INJUN BILL
This is my mission, Froggy!

FROGGY
What if the Governor ain't even there? What if Abel just said that to…

INJUN BILL
Don't say that! Don't you even think it! The time has come for all debts to be paid. And you don't wanna be around when that bill comes due.

FROGGY
Please let me come with you. Never had me a Denver Omelet. Like to give that a try.

INJUN BILL
No.

FROGGY
I'm begging you.

INJUN BILL
This town ain't half bad. Set up your restaurant, send for your mama and...

FROGGY
I can't, dammit! I got nothin' left! In a thunderbolt, it all got took away from me! My momma's gone and I'll never be able to look my sister in the eye and...

INJUN BILL
I'm resolved, Froggy. You stay here.

FROGGY
Well then I'm gonna follow you whether you want me to or not. And I'd like to see you stop me.

(BILL gets deadly serious)

FROGGY
Wait. No. I don't wanna see that.

INJUN BILL
Lemme tell you something. I don't give two

shits what happens to you, and I expect the same goddamn courtesy in return. You start followin' people around in this world, and they end up leading you straight to Hell.

FROGGY
I'd rather go to Hell with a friend then to Heaven by myself.

(INJUN BILL grabs him roughly)

INJUN BILL
We ain't friends! How many times I gotta tell you? Say it again and I'll cut your damn tongue out!

(BILL collects himself)

FROGGY
How you gettin' to Denver?

INJUN BILL
My own damn way.

FROGGY
All the way to Colorado? You best take the train.

INJUN BILL
Well, thank God Froggy's here to point out the goddamn obvious! I can't take the train 'cause I can't afford the train! Figure I'll steal a horse and...

(FROGGY walks off)

INJUN BILL
Well. There he goes.

(INJUN BILL opens his rations, eats some beef jerky)

INJUN BILL
Mm. Good jerky.

(FROGGY soon returns with two train tickets)

INJUN BILL
Aw, dammit all to hell... what're you doin' back?

FROGGY
Here. *(Gives him a ticket)*

INJUN BILL
What the hell is this?

FROGGY
Well, since clearly I'm just here to point out the obvious, them there's a train ticket.

INJUN BILL
Where'd you get it?

FROGGY
I said the magic words, reached right up my butthole and WOOP. Train tickets.

INJUN BILL
You steal these?

FROGGY
Of course I stole 'em. I'm good at stealin'.

INJUN BILL
You stole two of 'em.

FROGGY
Figure that out all by yourself.

INJUN BILL
Stop bustin' my balls, fat man!

(Beat. FROGGY smiles, laughs a little)

FROGGY
Bill, I don't know what happened your whole life. I'm guessin' you got kicked around more then's fair. But this is what people do.

INJUN BILL
They steal train tickets?

FROGGY
They help... sometimes for no good reason at all.

(INJUN BILL thinks on that)

FROGGY
What d'ya say? Am I in?

(Beat)

INJUN BILL
There's a crazy man out there killin' whole villages. I reckon I could use the backup.

FROGGY
Damn right.

(In the darkness, the sound of a hammer drawing back on a shotgun. The SHERIFF can be heard in the darkness)

SHERIFF
There's an old saying that goes "No snowflake falls in the wrong place."

(They turn, arms raised)

SHERIFF
And here are two snowflakes I thought I'd never see again, holdin' stolen tickets.

(He steps into the light)

SHERIFF
Ladies, you just rolled snake-eyes.

(Lights fade)

END OF ACT ONE

ACT II

Scene 1

ACTOR 2
(singing)
BROKE AND SHACKLED IN A TRAIN CAR,
BILL AND FROGGY SEEMED DEFEATED
'CAUSE THE SHERIFF, HE HAD GREETED THEM
WITH SMILES AND A GUN
SO THEY RODE OFF WITHOUT KNOWIN'
WHERE THE GODDAMN TRAIN WAS GOIN'
AND THEY HAD THAT SINKIN' FEELING
LIKE THEIR RACE WAS ALL BUT RUN

(Lights up. FROGGY & INJUN BILL sit in a train car. Their hands are bound. They bounce occasionally to indicate motion. FROGGY whimpers occasionally. INJUN BILL ignores it initially, but finally--)

INJUN BILL
What? What is it?

FROGGY
You got a cup or somethin'?

INJUN BILL
What do you think?

FROGGY
Bill, it's an emergency!

INJUN BILL
I ain't got no goddamn cup, Froggy! Christ.

FROGGY
Well, then...I'm real sorry about this.

(FROGGY dashes to BILL's side of the car and begins to undo his pants)

INJUN BILL
What the hell are you doin'?

FROGGY
I gotta piss, and I ain't gonna piss where I sit!

INJUN BILL
Don't.

FROGGY
I gotta!

INJUN BILL
I don't wanna smell your piss from here to wherever we're goin'!

FROGGY
Dammit! I can't get my damn pants off!

INJUN BILL
Just hold it!

FROGGY
No! That makes my pecker hurt!

(BILL gets up, grabs FROGGY and throws him back into his previous seat)

INJUN BILL
You're gonna hold it 'til the train stops. It ain't stopped yet today, so I reckon it's gonna soon.

FROGGY
Look, I'm not doin' this to spite you. This here's a bodily function with a will utterly independent of my wishes. *(He groans)* And I ain't about to ruin my one pair of pants.

INJUN BILL
You're thinkin' about it too much.

FROGGY
Well, Bill, it's like someone farting in Church. You can sit there, lookin' at your hymnal, singin' about The Virgin Jesus but all you're really thinkin' about is "Who the hell just farted in church?"

INJUN BILL
Pretty sure it was the Virgin Mary.

FROGGY
And I'm pretty sure I got a goddamn gorilla squeezin' my balls!

INJUN BILL
Here. *(Starts to rifle through FROGGY's pockets)*

FROGGY
Um... what... whatcha doin' there, Bill?

(INJUN BILL hands FROGGY his harmonica)

INJUN BILL
Play somethin'.

FROGGY
Come on!

INJUN BILL
It'll take your mind off your piss-pipe. Do it!

(FROGGY half-heartedly plays Swanee River. He begins to get into it. BILL perhaps sings along. He finishes the song, then just lies there for a bit)

FROGGY
Injun Bill?

INJUN BILL
Yep.

FROGGY
I regret playing a song about a river.

INJUN BILL
You gotta hold it in, son.

FROGGY
I'm worried that I'm doin' irreparable damage to my nethers as we speak.

INJUN BILL
You ain't. I gone two days without pissin' once. I'm fine.

FROGGY
You lie.

INJUN BILL
Hand to god. Remember that preacher I was in jail with?

FROGGY
The fella you told about the shoes?

INJUN BILL
That's him. Well, he was a talker. Never shut up. Went on and on about his family gettin' burned up

in Georgia, 'bout how God don't make no sense, bullshit like that. Problem was, he was sittin' on the pisspot the whole time. I was too damn drunk to knock him off it, so I just pinched it shut and waited.

FROGGY
How much time you spent in jail, Bill?

INJUN BILL
Enough.

FROGGY
That place where you and I met... that was my first time. Got me a drunk-on and tried to steal some horses.

INJUN BILL
While you was drunk?

FROGGY
Yep.

INJUN BILL
How many you try to steal?

(Beat)

FROGGY
The thing you gotta remember is rye whiskey can fuck a man up good.

INJUN BILL
How many?

FROGGY
It woulda been in the neighborhood of... fifteen. Twenty at the limit.

INJUN BILL
(chuckling) What did you do? Just open the gate

at the corral?

FROGGY
(starting to chuckle too) I swear to god, I thought it would work.

(They laugh together)

FROGGY
You think the sheriff's takin' us to jail?

INJUN BILL
Naw. We been on this train all day. He coulda dropped us off at a half-dozen towns.

FROGGY
Guess you're right.

INJUN BILL
I don't trust a man what speaks philosophy.

FROGGY
I don't like that he called us snowflakes.

INJUN BILL
What the hell did that even mean?

FROGGY
Got me. For a second, I thought I must've heard him wrong. Like maybe he was callin' us… pancakes.

INJUN BILL
Froggy, that makes less sense than callin' us snowflakes.

FROGGY
I think it makes exactly as much sense. *(Beat)* Now I want pancakes.

INJUN BILL
Me too.

FROGGY
Drippin' with syrup.

INJUN BILL
And bacon.

FROGGY
Yes. Hell yes. A whole pigs-worth.

INJUN BILL
Nice and crispy.

FROGGY
But not burned.

INJUN BILL
Nope. Done up right so's they crunch, but they ain't burned.

(They lie back, enjoying the thought)

INJUN BILL
Hey, Froggy.

FROGGY
Yes'm?

INJUN BILL
What's it like to want somethin'?

(Beat)

FROGGY
Like bacon?

INJUN BILL
No, I mean... to want somethin' more than... essentials. Like... what's it like wantin' to start up a restaurant?

FROGGY
Bill, that particular dream's gone tits-up.

INJUN BILL
Before then. Before you let it go. What's it like?

FROGGY
(Thinking on that) Like fuel for the furnace of your heart.

INJUN BILL
(smiling a bit) That sounds nice.

FROGGY
Sure enough. Keeps you goin' when there ain't no reason to go on. Like you know that if you can just hang on a little longer, that your luck'll change. That you won't end up some fat drunk who damn-near ramrods his own sister.

(Beat)

INJUN BILL
What?

FROGGY
I'm just sayin'… havin' a dream matters. Matters more than anything. *(FROGGY looks at INJUN BILL)* Ain't you never had somethin' like that?

(Beat)

INJUN BILL
I'm gonna kill the man that wears my friend as shoes.

FROGGY
That ain't a dream. That's a mission. What do you dream about?

INJUN BILL
I don't know.

FROGGY
When you pray to god "God, please gimme this one thing so that I got a reason to roll my ass outta bed"… what is it you pray for?

(BILL thinks on that)

FROGGY
OK. So let's say you kill this Osborne fella. What're you gonna do after that?

INJUN BILL
I ain't thought it out that far.

FROGGY
Bill, you gotta figure out what makes you happy.

INJUN BILL
Not sure I ever been happy.

FROGGY
I'm tellin' you. One day, something's gonna happen to you, somethin' so beautiful it's gonna take your breath away. Then you'll know what I'm talkin' about.

INJUN BILL
Pffft.

FROGGY
It ain't that hard. Just gotta take time to smell the flowers is all.

(INJUN BILL laughs a sad laugh)
FROGGY
What?

INJUN BILL
I ain't never even smelled a flower.

(The train stops. The SHERIFF walks over)

SHERIFF
Last stop, ladies! Don't make me get the railroad bulls!

(FROGGY jumps down and runs offstage. The SHERIFF goes for his gun)

INJUN BILL
He ain't runnin' off, Sheriff. He just has to piss somethin' awful.

SHERIFF
(calling off-stage) Piss where you stand, Baptiste. That way I can see ya.

FROGGY
(calling from off-stage) I can't do it if you're watchin'!

SHERIFF
Make fuckin' do! *(To INJUN BILL)* Injun Bill Picote.

(Beat)

INJUN BILL
I don't actually know your name.

SHERIFF
Sheriff J.B. Abernathy, at your service. Well, not Sheriff anymore. I resigned that lofty position when last we saw each other.

INJUN BILL
You mean when you left us for dead?

SHERIFF
No, what I give you was but one of many tests. Gettin' yourselves free? You passed that one. I'd hoped that your sudden liberty would have set

you on a path to greatness. I cannot tell you the disappointment I felt seeing you and the Cajun back to your larcenous ways.

SHERIFF
(calling off-stage) You about done there, sport?

FROGGY
Don't rush me!

INJUN BILL
I never asked nothin' of you.

SHERIFF
True enough, true enough. But still, I gave it to you. And you know why? 'Cause you two buttflaps are my lucky charms.

(FROGGY returns)

FROGGY
Oh sweet merciful Christ. I think I coulda filled the Grand Canyon.

SHERIFF
C'mon over here, Froggy.

(FROGGY crosses to him. SHERIFF puts his arms around the two prisoners)

SHERIFF
Ladies, it wasn't so long ago that I was just some sheriff in a pisspot town, and you was my prisoners. I have since then elevated my station, and you, sadly, have not.

FROGGY
Ain't life a kick in the nuts.

SHERIFF
Oh, it can be. No denying that. But not if you

hang on to hope. My hope was sending my wife and son down here to run my brother's claim. Poor Jeremiah got himself the small pox and passed, so the mine went to me. That telegram I got? Turns out my boy struck gold. *(throws his arms wide)* Welcome to Denver, city of dreams!

INJUN BILL
Wait, what?

SHERIFF
We have arrived at the land of my fortune.

INJUN BILL
Denver? We're in Denver?!

FROGGY
I'll be damned.

SHERIFF
That's right. Can't you smell the gold in the air? *(He breathes deeply)* That's the smell of a new life! Like the mighty phoenix, I am reborn!

FROGGY
Wait. Are we in Denver or Phoenix?

SHERIFF
Now, I reckon you're wondering why I dragged you all the way to Colorado. Well... I'm here to offer you another kindness. I'm puttin' you two butt-flaps to work in my mine!

INJUN BILL
Now hold on...

SHERIFF
I figured you'd probably try to run off if I didn't drag you down here by force. But this... this is your chance to make a real life for yourself.

Honest work at an honest wage. No more thieving and drinking and whoring... boys, you don't have to thank me.

(Beat)

FROGGY
Thank you?

SHERIFF
Oh, it's the least I could do.

INJUN BILL
Sheriff, you gotta let us go.

(Beat. The SHERIFF looks at him)

SHERIFF
Is that a fact?

INJUN BILL
You got us in the crosshairs, and I ain't about to argue it. But the hand of destiny is at work here. I can feel it.

SHERIFF
Can you?

INJUN BILL
When you caught us pick-pocketin'...

FROGGY
Allegedly pick-pocketin'...

INJUN BILL
...it was so we could make it to Denver. And now... here we are. That's gotta mean something.

SHERIFF
And what is it you seek to do here in Denver?

INJUN BILL
I'm gonna find my destiny! I been chasin' it for two long years and…

SHERIFF
Now, son. You're speakin' in vagaries.

INJUN BILL.
I mean to settle a great injustice.

SHERIFF
That don't strike me as your long suit.

INJUN BILL
I'm a bad man, sir. I admit that with no hesitation. But a horrible thing been done to the last man on Earth I called "friend."

SHERIFF
Froggy?

INJUN BILL
No.

FROGGY
Thanks.

INJUN BILL
And the man what done this wrong is coming to Denver. Here is where we shall finally meet, face to face.

SHERIFF
Yeah? And what are you gonna do then?

INJUN BILL
I mean to kill him, if that's what you're asking.

SHERIFF
In so many words.

INJUN BILL
I need this, sir. I need it like a fish needs water and a fat man needs cake.

FROGGY
Hey! Are you…?

INJUN BILL
But you have my word on this, Sheriff. Once I see this man dead, my killin' days are over. I'll find somethin' else to do with my life. Somethin'… decent. But this vengeance needs doin' first.

(The SHERIFF stares hard at INJUN BILL)

FROGGY
I'd like to go on record as mostly just bein' in the wrong place at the wrong time.

SHERIFF
This man you mean to kill… what'd he do exactly?

INJUN BILL
He took my dead friend, skinned him, and turned him into shoes.

FROGGY
And now he's Governor of Wyoming.

SHERIFF
Sweet Jesus. I don't know which is worse. *(He uncuffs BILL & FROGGY)*

SHERIFF
If the devil were to open his eyes slowly enough, no one would even notice he'd awakened.

FROGGY
Come again?

SHERIFF
That's a bit of J.B.'s own personal philosophy. Fact is, the world we live in gets worse every single day, but it does it little by little so most don't notice. I do my part to correct the growing wickedness in the world with small acts of goodness.

FROGGY
That's right kind of you, but…

SHERIFF
I see before me a wicked man who may just recant if he can right this single injustice. Tell me, Injun Bill. Do I assess this correctly?

(Beat)

INJUN BILL
Yuh-huh.

SHERIFF
Then who am I to stand in the way of redemption?

(Both men are now free)

FROGGY
You lettin' us go?

SHERIFF
You must be the brains of the operation. *(He digs into his wallet, gives them some money)*

SHERIFF
Here's the bills we took off of you back in Montana, minus my fee for hauling you here. Not much, but I reckon two resourceful butt-flaps like yourselves will find a way.

(BILL looks at the money, then offers the SHERIFF his hand)

INJUN BILL
Thank you, Sheriff.

SHERIFF
It's just J.B. now, son.

(FROGGY shakes his other hand)

FROGGY
Sir, if you was a woman, I reckon I'd kiss you full on the mouth.

SHERIFF
Then praise Jesus for my cock and balls.

INJUN BILL
C'mon, Froggy.

(BILL grabs him and starts to head off)

SHERIFF
Swing on over to my claim, let me know how things turn out!

INJUN BILL
Yessir!

FROGGY
Full on the mouth!

(He watches them leave, then takes another deep breath of the air and smiles)

SHERIFF
"Gold is tried by fire, brave men by adversity." I believe a Greek fella said that.

(He exits. Lights fade)

Scene 2

ACTOR 1
(singing)
INJUN BILL, INJUN BILL
AS YOUR PREY GROWS EVER NEARER,
IS YOUR VISION GETTING CLEARER,
OR DOES HATE STILL CLOUD YOUR EYES?
INJUN BILL, REST YOUR BONES
AT THE FIRST FLOPHOUSE YOU COME TO
'CAUSE THERE'S NOWHERE LEFT TO RUN TO
AS YOU CLOSE IN ON YOUR PRIZE

(The interior of the 4-Room Hotel. It is a cramped, decrepit place. A check-in desk stands at one side, a small table w/ two chairs stands in the other. FROGGY & INJUN BILL enter. FROGGY has an apple. A white hat hangs on a post)

INJUN BILL
Christ, what a shithole.

FROGGY
You said you wanted the cheapest hotel in town.

This is it.

INJUN BILL
I seen bigger closets.

FROGGY
I'll bring it up with the management. *(looks around)* Where the hell's the management?

INJUN BILL
Place looks deserted.

FROGGY
Well, it's on the outskirts.

INJUN BILL
I don't know. Rest of the town seems full to over-flowin'.

(Beat)

FROGGY
Bill. I'm havin' a bad thought.

INJUN BILL
Yeah?

FROGGY
What if that Death fella was here? What if he killed all that was in it, and ain't no one noticed yet?

INJUN BILL
Quit jumpin' at shadows.

FROGGY
The man what sold me this apple... he said a pale rider's been seen 'round these parts. Sometimes he wipes out a whole village, sometimes just a few people. And no one's been able to catch him.

INJUN BILL
Not my concern.

FROGGY
Gimme a knife.

INJUN BILL
No.

FROGGY
I need to defend myself.

INJUN BILL
You got that apple.

FROGGY
I got...?! What the hell am I supposed to do with this? Spit seeds at him?!

INJUN BILL
I killed a man with a plum once. I reckon the principle's pretty much the same.

FROGGY
You're a lyin' sack of crap.

(INJUN BILL glares at him)

FROGGY
You know what? I didn't... you're not a sack. *(grabs the chairs and uses them to pin the door shut)*

INJUN BILL
For Christ's sake...

FROGGY
I'm tellin' you, Death is comin'. I feel it in my bones. We gotta be ready.

INJUN BILL
I'm always ready.

FROGGY
Well, I ain't. C'mon, give me a knife.

INJUN BILL
No.

FROGGY
Just a little one.

INJUN BILL
No.

FROGGY
How's about Quiet Annie? She ain't no bigger than...

INJUN BILL
Listen up. My knives are precious to me. Especially Annie. If someone comes for ya, I'll take care of him.

FROGGY
You'd do that for me?

INJUN BILL
A dog defends the fleas on him, even if he don't mean to.

FROGGY
Thank you, Bill.

INJUN BILL
De nada. *(He sits down, smiling)*

FROGGY
Ain't you the cat that ate the canary.

INJUN BILL
Osbourne's here, Froggy. I know it. I know it more than I ever knew anything else. Two years of hunting.... livin' in caves and hidin' in alleys

and followin' every trail, even if... it don't matter. None of it matters no more, 'cause he's here. My quest is all but over. Death himself couldn't stop me.

(The back door shakes. FROGGY lets out a girlish scream. INJUN BILL draws his saber)

FROGGY
Save me, Jesus!

(The back door opens. MARTHA enters with a mop and bucket. She sees them and lets out a startled cry)

MARTHA
Oh my goodness!

FROGGY
DEAAAAAATH!

(INJUN BILL sheathes his blade quickly. MARTHA pulls a gun on them)

MARTHA
What do you want?!

INJUN BILL
Beggin' your pardon, Miss. We didn't mean to startle you.

(FROGGY checks the front of his pants for wetness. There is none)

FROGGY
...oh, thank god...

INJUN BILL
We're just arrived in town, and lookin' for accommodations.

MARTHA
With a saber drawn?

INJUN BILL
There's bad folks around, Miss. We was afraid you was one of 'em.

(She examines them for a bit, then lowers the gun)

MARTHA
All right then.

INJUN BILL
Again, real sorry about the fright.

MARTHA
Quite all right. I'm fine.

INJUN BILL
Is your husband around? Mayhap we should…

MARTHA
My husband passed five years ago. This is my place now.

(Beat. FROGGY looks around, taking in the disheveled décor)

FROGGY
And a fine establishment it is.

MARTHA
You say you're looking for a room?

INJUN BILL
Two rooms, miss. I can't emphasize that enough.

MARTHA
Just… here it is… *(She pulls out a ledger)* Please sign your name here.

(INJUN BILL looks at it, then to FROGGY)

INJUN BILL
I... um... Froggy, could you...?

FROGGY
Yessir. *(signs them in)*

MARTHA
Froggy? Your name is Froggy?

FROGGY
It's what ya call a pseudo... pseudo... psu... nickname.

MARTHA
I should hope so, Mr... *(checks the ledger)* Baptiste?

FROGGY
C'est vrais.

MARTHA
So that must make you... *(checks the ledger again)* Mr. Custer?

INJUN BILL
(glaring at FROGGY) I guess it must.

MARTHA
Well, you're in luck. I'm sorry to say we have many vacancies at the moment. In so much as you two would be my first real guests in three weeks.

FROGGY
Well, you got someone signed up here. Ber-Tram Shaw.

MARTHA
I'd hardly call him a real guest. He checked in last night and paid me in fool's gold. As soon as he returns, I'm tossing him out on his ear.

FROGGY
Sounds like you've had a bad run of things.

MARTHA
Yes. My husband built this hotel ten years ago. When the bigger, fancier ones popped up in the center of town, we couldn't compete. We also couldn't afford to renovate, so... here I am.

FROGGY
I'm real sorry to hear that, miss.

MARTHA
Oh, I make do somehow. The rates are five dollars a night, with two upfront.

(FROGGY gets the money)

MARTHA
And just how long will you gentlemen be staying with us?

INJUN BILL
Well, ma'am, that all depends. We're waitin' for someone. So we're here until he arrives.

MARTHA
Really?

INJUN BILL
Yes, ma'am.

MARTHA
I hope you don't mind my saying I'll pray for a delay in his arrival.

(INJUN BILL just stares at her)

MARTHA
Because... then you'll have to stay here longer. And I'd make more money.

(INJUN BILL continues staring)

MARTHA
It... it was a joke.

FROGGY
Sorry, miss. Mr. Custer here was born without a sense of humor.

MARTHA
I see. I hope you don't mind my asking, but are you by chance related to the great General Custer?

(Beat)

INJUN BILL
Distantly.

MARTHA
Isn't that remarkable? *(She produces two keys)* I'll give you gentlemen rooms 1 and 2. The small dining area there is open to you. I'm sorry to say I have no food, but there's plenty of liquor. If I may be of further service, within the limits of Christian decency, please let me know.

INJUN BILL
Well, since you brung it up... You ever hear the name Dr. John Eugene Osborne?

MARTHA
I can't say that I have. Is he the gentleman you're waiting on?

INJUN BILL
And that's a fact.

MARTHA
Well, I'll certainly keep my ears open for his

arrival. And please know that I was only joking about the...

FROGGY
He knows... don't you... um... Filbert?

(INJUN BILL glares at him again)

INJUN BILL
I reckon I do.

FROGGY
Well, I'm headin' on up. I feel like I ain't slept on a real bed since never.

INJUN BILL
You're in #2.

FROGGY
How's that?

INJUN BILL
I'm in charge, so I'm in #1. Got it?

FROGGY
...don't make no difference which...

MARTHA
Oh! Mr. Custer!

(INJUN BILL continues upstairs)

MARTHA
Mr. Custer!

(FROGGY turns him around)

FROGGY
I believe the young lady is addressing you, Filbert. You must forgive him. He's... um... he's deaf in one ear.

MARTHA
Oh. I'm sorry.

(She raises her voice to an uncomfortable level)

MARTHA
The gentleman you were referring to - John Eugene Osborne?

INJUN BILL
Yeah.

MARTHA
Is he some sort of politician? From Wyoming? Thick moustache, glasses...?

INJUN BILL
(lighting up) Yes! Oh god yes! Is he here?! Where's he stayin'?

MARTHA
Mr. Custer... Doctor Osborne came and went a week ago.

(INJUN BILL freezes. He remains immobile except for a twitching eye. He then turns & walks into the other room. He then screams loudly in unbridled rage. MARTHA jumps. FROGGY desperately tries to cover)

FROGGY
He... um... ah... kidney stone.

(Lights fade)

Scene 3

(The next day, still at the hotel. INJUN BILL is in the dining area, his head on the table. A variety of bottles are around him. FROGGY enters from his room)

FROGGY
Lord, Bill. How much can a man drink in one night?

(FROGGY shakes him. BILL mumbles something incomprehensible and pushes FROGGY away)

FROGGY
C'mon, partner. Let's....

(FROGGY tries to lift BILL. BILL again mumbles and punches FROGGY in the gut. FROGGY stumbles back, more shocked than hurt)

FROGGY
Fine! Just sit there and pickle in your own juices for all I care!

(Beat. FROGGY sits down with him)

FROGGY
I didn't mean that. I was speakin' out of hurt.

(INJUN BILL mumbles)

FROGGY
Here's the thing, Bill. Time's come where we gotta figure out our next move. I figure you wanna get back on the hunt, but I don't wanna do nothin' without your say-so. 'Cause.... I gotta say, there are reasons to stay put. We got a real job with the Sheriff. Got a roof over our head, for a little while anyways. Now I know Big Nose George was your friend, but...

(INJUN BILL suddenly sits straight up)

INJUN BILL
You know what?! George Parrot was a son of a bitch! *(He takes a long drink out of a bottle, then slams his head back on the table)*

FROGGY
Well. Guess I'll try again tomorrow.

(MARTHA enters from the back room, and starts dusting the desk)

MARTHA
Good morning, Mr. Baptiste.

FROGGY
Mornin', Ms. Barnes. And please, it's Froggy.

MARTHA
Then I must insist you call me Martha. How fares your friend?

FROGGY
Less than sober.

MARTHA
I understand. My Walter had a kidney stone once. Liquor was the only thing that kept the pain at bay. In the end, it took his life.

FROGGY
Oh. I'm sorry. I…

MARTHA
It's quite all right. Ours was a marriage of convenience.

FROGGY
My momma said weren't nothin' convenient about marriage. 'Course my papa was a gator farmer, so…

MARTHA
My people were farmers too, but our crops withered in a drought, like a biblical famine of old. Walter was a family friend, and he took me in.

FROGGY
Don't sound real romantic, if you pardon my sayin'.

MARTHA
As I said, convenience, not romance. I was sixteen when I married. Walter was… much older.

FROGGY
Yeah, it's a bitch, but… Oh, I'm sorry.

MARTHA
It's quite all right. I'm no stranger to salty language, though I may not speak it myself.

FROGGY
You're a real proper lady.

MARTHA
I am what I was raised to be.

(FROGGY has gone back to BILL. He tries to remove a bottle from BILL's hand, but fails)

MARTHA
You're very loyal to your friend.

FROGGY
I suppose.

MARTHA
Do you mind if I ask why?

FROGGY
Filbert here... Life's dealt him every shit card in the deck. So I figure, give the poor som'bitch a hand when I can.

MARTHA
That's very big of you.

FROGGY
You callin' me fat?

MARTHA
What? No, not at all.

FROGGY
Oh. Sorry, I... it's a sore subject.

(She just stares at him. He grows a bit uncomfortable)

FROGGY
I... do I have something on my face?

MARTHA
I was just... if you're going to say here another night, I'll need another five dollars. From each

of you.

FROGGY
Oh... ah, shit... I mean, shoot... I mean...

MARTHA
You're financial state is...?

FROGGY
To be honest, Miss, it's... bleak.

MARTHA
I see.

FROGGY
Me and Bill...

MARTHA
Bill?

FROGGY
Filbert... we're not men of means, if you gather my meaning.

MARTHA
I believe I do.

FROGGY
Well.... all right then.

(FROGGY tries to lift BILL. BILL leaps up and shouts a string of nonsense at him)

INJUN BILL
Fuck off you cocksucking motherfucker touch me again and I won't but you will so stop all you're you know what I don't have to take this from mommy doesn't...!!!

(INJUN BILL collapses, unconscious)

MARTHA
Oh my.

FROGGY
Sorry. He's an... interesting drunk.

MARTHA
Mr. Ba... Froggy, might I make a suggestion?

FROGGY
Sure enough.

MARTHA
I just... it's been nice having a masculine presence here. You, I mean. It's been nice having you here.

FROGGY
Thank you, miss.

MARTHA
And as you've likely noticed, my hotel is... in need of repair.

FROGGY
I've seen worse.

MARTHA
Really?

FROGGY
Well, not much worse.

MARTHA
So perhaps we can come to an... arrangement?

FROGGY
Um... I can play the harmonica.

MARTHA
Can you swing a hammer?

FROGGY
Sure.

MARTHA
Do you know anything about roofs?

FROGGY
Not really, but I'm a fast learner! *(Beat)* That's not true. I ain't real bright. But...

MARTHA
What I'm proposing, Froggy, is that... perhaps if you and your friend would agree to some manual labor, then I could forgo your payment for a short time.

FROGGY
Ma'am... I don't know what to say. That's about the kindest offer I've gotten since the Army kicked me out.

MARTHA
Then you agree?

FROGGY
It would be my pleasure.

MARTHA
Good.

FROGGY
And if you'd like... I used to be a cook. I can make shoe leather taste like sirloin.

MARTHA
Really?

FROGGY
Yes, ma'am. You like shrimp? Or crawdads?

MARTHA
Oh! Very much!

FROGGY
Martha, you give me ten minutes with your kitchen and you'll think you're in the French Quarter!

MARTHA
Oh, Froggy! That sounds lovely! *(She touches his hand)* Thank you.

(They realize their hands are touching, and she removes her hand quickly. FROGGY finally realizes her intent)

FROGGY
Oh. My.

MARTHA
I'm sorry. I didn't mean to be so forward.

FROGGY
Shucks, Martha. It's all right.

MARTHA
My mother would be mortified.

FROGGY
Ain't no reason.

MARTHA
I'll just get to my cleaning and...

(She starts to go. FROGGY takes her hand and holds it. They smile at each other)

FROGGY
See? Ain't no harm in this, is there?

MARTHA
No. I suppose not.

FROGGY
Now, I'm gonna head to the market square real quick like. See if I can wrangle up some food.

MARTHA
I thought you had no money.

(FROGGY grabs the white hat)

FROGGY
This belong to that Bertram fella?

MARTHA
Yes.

FROGGY
Well, since he played you rotten with that fool's gold, maybe I'll sell this. Bet I can get a half-decent price for it.

MARTHA
But it's not yours.

FROGGY
I won't tell if you don't.

(He puts it on, then tips it to her)

FROGGY
Ma'am.

(He leaves. She stands there for a bit, smiling)

MARTHA
Oh, Martha. Why do you always fall for the dangerous ones?

(Lights fade)

Scene 4

ACTOR 2
(singing)
IN THE THOROUGHFARE OF DENVER,
FROGGY WALKED & FROGGY PONDERED
AND THE MORE THAT HIS MIND WANDERED,
THE MORE QUESTIONS WOULD ARISE
BUT THE ANSWERS KEPT REFUSIN'
TO GIVE HIM JUST ONE CONCLUSION
'TIL A FRIEND INSIDE A PLAGUE TENT
OFFERED TO PHILOSOPHIZE

(A plague tent in the Denver Thoroughfare. The SHERIFF lies inside, moaning. His face is pock marked. FROGGY walks by, still wearing the hat. He soon comes back and looks in)

FROGGY
Sheriff Abernathy?

(FROGGY enters. The SHERIFF sees him)

SHERIFF
Stay away, son. I've got the pox.

FROGGY
I ain't worried. I got the shot when I was in the Army.

SHERIFF
Then you're a luckier soul than I.

FROGGY
Sweet Jesus. What happened to you?

(Beat)

SHERIFF
Remember ten seconds ago, when I told you I got the pox?

FROGGY
Right. Sorry, I... right.

(The sound of coughing/moaning from elsewhere)

FROGGY
This is a hell of a place for a rich man to end up.

SHERIFF
That's the one admirable trait of Pestilence. It can't be bought off.

FROGGY
You don't look so bad.

SHERIFF
Then my external appearance does not reflect my internal concerns. My back hurts so much I can barely breathe. Can't seem to stop sweatin', even though I'm cold as a... as a... Jesus Christ. I can't even think of a fuckin' simile.

FROGGY
Hold up a second. *(FROGGY exits, then soon returns with a cup of water)* Here you go. Drink up.

(The SHERIFF drinks a little, but starts coughing)

FROGGY
You just hang in there, Sheriff. I seen men beat the pox before.

SHERIFF
I am nothing if not an optimist.

FROGGY
I don't know what to say, sir. I'm sorry as hell.

SHERIFF
No, no, no. Don't you be feelin' sorry for me. I'm still basking in good luck's graces.

(Beat)

FROGGY
I...think that maybe what you think is lucky and what I think is lucky ain't the same thing.

SHERIFF
You can't let a thing like the pox get you down. Beyond the literal inability to get up, that is.

FROGGY
I can't tell if you're really this cheerful, or if the fever's cooked your brains.

SHERIFF
Somethin' stuck in your craw, son?

FROGGY
Ah, just thinkin' is all.

SHERIFF
Hell, son! That's ol' J.B.'s favorite pastime!

(The SHERIFF sits up, puts his arm around FROGGY, who is clearly uncomfortable)

SHERIFF
Tell me what's on your mind, Froggy.

FROGGY
Well, sir. I feel like maybe I'm at one of them road-forks.

SHERIFF
Mm-hmm.

FROGGY
On one side, I got Bill. That fella he's after.... som'bitch got away from us.

SHERIFF
Lord, lord.

FROGGY
So I reckon we'll be hittin' the road soon, back on the trail. And I know it ain't my mission, but... Bill needs someone to watch his back. There's some crazy bastard out there burnin' through the West like a brushfire.

SHERIFF
So you want to protect your friend. A noble motivation. So what's on the other side of the fork?

(FROGGY mumbles & blushes, embarrassed)

SHERIFF
Is it a woman?

(FROGGY mumbles again)

SHERIFF
Hot damn, son! In Denver for all of two days, and you got yourself a sweetheart!

FROGGY
Oh, it ain't all that. It's the Widow Barnes, over to the 4-Room Hotel.

SHERIFF
But you're sweet on her?

FROGGY
I reckon.

SHERIFF
And is the Widow equally enamored?

FROGGY
Well, we spent all last night just talkin', while Bill tore through the liquor. It was real... nice.

SHERIFF
Makes ya feel like stayin' put, don't it?

(FROGGY nods)

SHERIFF
How long's it been since you been with a woman?

FROGGY
Over a year now. Less'n you count when I damn near ram-rodded my own sister.

(Beat. SHERIFF removes his arm)

SHERIFF
Maybe you don't mention that to the Widow.

FROGGY
So now I'm feelin' kinda...split in two.

SHERIFF
Remember when I told you before about the rabbits? That's where you are again... chasin' two and catching neither. I reckon what you need to do is decide which one's the one you really wanna sink your teeth into.

FROGGY
Huh. I just now figured out what that meant.

SHERIFF
The best philosophy is like real good chaw. You gotta chew on it for a while to really appreciate the flavor.

(FROGGY laughs. The SHERIFF pulls a gold rock out of his pocket & hands it to FROGGY)

FROGGY
Hot damn!

SHERIFF
You take that rock, and you cash it out. Buy your lady some flowers and a nice meal. All I ask is that you have yourself one romantic evening before you make your decision.

FROGGY
I can't take this, sir. It's too much.

SHERIFF
I got a mine full of 'em. Take it with my blessing.

FROGGY
I gotta be honest. I don't know why you keep helping me out, but...

SHERIFF
A smarter feller than me once said "Be kind, for everyone you meet is fighting a harder battle." *(He*

claps FROGGY shoulder, then coughs)

FROGGY
Ah, I'm an ass. Pissin' in your ear while you're the one in the plague tent.

SHERIFF
You gave me a chance to philosophize, Froggy. That's a fine gift.

FROGGY
Is there anything I can do for you?

SHERIFF
Well, you got a little time?

FROGGY
Yessir.

SHERIFF
I'd sure take it kindly if you played on that mouth harp. I find it... soothing.

FROGGY
That I can do. You wanna hear anything in particular?

SHERIFF
Something... felicitous.

(Beat. FROGGY has no idea what that word means)

FROGGY
Okie-doke.

(FROGGY plays. The SHERIFF lays back down and smiles. Lights fade)

Scene 5

ACTOR 1
(singing)
Injun Bill, Injun Bill
Sing the darkest Hallelujah
Let the knives that whisper to ya
Keep the promise of the past
Injun Bill, Injun Bill
Feel the chill of the shadow
On your shoulder
'Cause the night grows ever colder,
And the Devil's come at last

(Back at the hotel, early evening of the same day. INJUN BILL is exactly where he was before. He's asleep, though clearly having a bad dream. After a bit of twitching & mumbling, he bolts straight up)

INJUN BILL
Oh god! M'face is melting! *(He looks around, coming to his senses. He rubs his face)*

INJUN BILL
Christ, my head...

(MARTHA enters. She is slightly more made up, with a flower in her hair)

MARTHA
Froggy? I... oh.

INJUN BILL
Miss... Miss... dammit. I forgot your name.

MARTHA
Ms. Barnes.

INJUN BILL
(He tips his hat) Ma'am.

MARTHA
I see you've come to.

INJUN BILL
That matter's up for debate.

MARTHA
You must have come down here last night. With the exception of some explosive profanity, you've been unconscious for the better part of a day.

(INJUN BILL sits down, drinks from a bottle)

MARTHA
I'm not sure more alcohol is the appropriate remedy.

INJUN BILL
I'll take that into consideration, doctor.

MARTHA
I'm not a doctor.

INJUN BILL
Then I guessed it. *(He rises, still a bit shaky & hung-over)* You took my reason for living.

MARTHA
I'm sorry?

INJUN BILL
No need. I ain't blamin' you. Just a messenger. But now... *(He laughs a bit)* How many times you gotta get your jaw broke before you walk out of the fight?

MARTHA
I'm not sure I...

INJUN BILL
I just... this thing's been eatin' up my life for two years. Time's come to let it go, but I don't know how. Part of me wants to be free of it worse'n anything, but the other part... You think I got one more punch in me, lady?

MARTHA
I'm afraid I don't really follow, Mr. Custer.

INJUN BILL
No. I reckon you don't.

(He tries to sit down, but slams into the table. MARTHA rushes forward to stable him and to rescue the bottles. This is the first time we've seen her out from behind the counter BILL stumbles, falls to her feet. He realizes that she's wearing a pair of men's shoes)

MARTHA
Oh my. Look at this mess.

INJUN BILL
Where you get them shoes?

MARTHA
I beg your...?

(He grabs her ankles)

MARTHA
Oh!

INJUN BILL
These.... oh my god... these are...

MARTHA
Unhand me!

(INJUN BILL rises. He is now very sober and grim)

INJUN BILL
Them shoes don't seem real ladylike.

MARTHA
That isn't any of....

INJUN BILL
If you tell me this ain't my concern, I will cut your throat, I swear to Christ.

(MARTHA backs away from him, terrified. She bumps into the desk)

INJUN BILL
I ain't gonna ask again. Where you get them shoes?

MARTHA
Please... please don't...

INJUN BILL
Them's the governor's shoes, ain't they? The man from Wyoming?

(She doesn't answer)

INJUN BILL
AIN'T THEY!?

(She nods, trying to keep from crying)

INJUN BILL
Good. You keep your mouth shut. Good. *(He rubs his eyes, trying to decide what to do)* I made a promise, woman. I swore I'd kill the man wearing those shoes. And now... here they are. And here you are. *(He draws his saber. She is about to scream)* Don't scream. You hear me? Screamin' is gonna force my hand.

MARTHA
Then...then you might not kill me?

(INJUN BILL has no response)

MARTHA
If you want the shoes, they're yours. Please, just take them.

INJUN BILL
It's bigger than that. Bigger than you or me or... *(Beat)* Them shoes is a friend of mine.

MARTHA
They belong to a friend of yours?

INJUN BILL
They don't belong to him. They are him.

(MARTHA sits there, confused)

INJUN BILL
You're wearin' shoes made from a dead man. My friend. They tore the skin off of his corpse and stitched him into... those things.

MARTHA
That's impossible.

INJUN BILL
You're wearin' my dead friend George on your goddamn feet!

MARTHA
(Removing the shoes) Please. Just take them. Here.

INJUN BILL
That ain't enough, woman! It ain't enough just to have 'em! A wrong has got to be righted!

MARTHA
I've done nothing!

INJUN BILL
Then why you got the shoes!?

(Beat. MARTHA slowly rises)

MARTHA
A week ago... when Dr. Osborne's coach was leaving. It rode past my hotel. One of his suitcases fell off and... I have nothing. Do you understand that? No food, no money... all my clothes were moth-eaten and... The day before, I had boiled and eaten my own shoes. I'd had no food for days and...when I found the Governor's bag, I knew it was a gift from God. I used his suits to mend my dresses. I used his stockings to warm my feet. And yes, I took his shoes and made them my own. I am not proud of these actions, Mr. Custer, but I'd do them again.

INJUN BILL
Picote. My name ain't Custer. It's Bill Picote.

MARTHA
Injun Bill Picote?

(He nods)

MARTHA
I've heard of you. You rob stagecoaches.

INJUN BILL
I do.

MARTHA
And you're a killer.

INJUN BILL
I am.

MARTHA
But... I'm a woman.

INJUN BILL
I killed women before.

MARTHA
For stealing a suitcase? For taking shoes to cover her bloody feet?

INJUN BILL
It's bigger than that, goddammit! *(He takes a beat to collect himself)* I'll do it gentle, I promise. I'll put the knife in the Sweet Spot. You won't even feel it go in. You'll just bleed out nice and easy. It's like fallin' asleep.

MARTHA
(Starting to weep) You don't have to! You can just walk away.

INJUN BILL
I can't.

MARTHA
Please!

INJUN BILL
No. I've been on this path for two years. This is where it has led me. God help me, I gotta end this.

(He closes on her. She tries to fight him off)

MARTHA
Stop!

INJUN BILL
NO! Stop telling me to… Just lie down and make this easy on yourself!

(She strikes him hard. He staggers back)

MARTHA
Don't you see how ridiculous this is?! I didn't do this to your friend! I gave you the shoes! Just leave!

INJUN BILL
I can't, goddammit! I made a promise, and the only way it ends is bloody! You set a date with my knives the minute you laced them shoes up.

MARTHA
Take the shoes, give them a proper burial, and this will be over and done.

INJUN BILL
It'll never be done. Not unless I spill blood. Don't you understand that?

MARTHA
I am innocent!

INJUN BILL
Ain't no one innocent! Not here, not now, not

ever! We're all of us up to our knees in blood and filth and... and... A MAN IS NOT SHOES!!!

(MARTHA clings to the wall in fear)

INJUN BILL
Do you hear me, you miserable shitpile of a world?! A Man! IS NOT! SHOES!!!

(He collapses, overwhelmed by his own emotion. MARTHA stands there frozen. After a long beat she rises, taking him the shoes)

MARTHA
I'm sorry for your loss. I am. But don't let it turn you into someone you're not.

INJUN BILL
You don't know who I am.

MARTHA
I know who Froggy is. And I know he stands by you no matter how roughly you treat him. That makes me think perhaps there's something better to you than the life you've lived.

(She hands the shoes to INJUN BILL. As soon as he touches them, a change comes over him. He stares at the shoes)

INJUN BILL
George? *(He looks at the shoes, then to MARTHA)* This is my friend. This is George.

MARTHA
I know.

INJUN BILL
He... used to be a lot bigger.

MARTHA
I can imagine.

INJUN BILL
I think... I think part of me never thought I'd see him again. But here he is and... *(He looks at the shoes again)* I'm sorry, George. I'm sorry you got killed on account of somethin' I did. And that some bastard doctor turned you into this. You were a shitheel, a loudmouth and a liar, but didn't deserve this. *(The truth of that hits him. He looks up at her)* You don't deserve this neither.

(MARTHA nearly collapses with relief)

MARTHA
Thank you.

INJUN BILL
Could you... I'm sorry to ask, but did I leave any liquor left?

MARTHA
One bottle. *(She gives him the bottle)* You wish to say goodbye to your friend.

(He nods)

MARTHA
Then I'll leave you to it. I find I could use some fresher air. *(Before she heads off--)* Froggy said that life has been less than kind to you. I know what that's like.

INJUN BILL
Froggy's an all right sort.

MARTHA
Yes. He is.

(She exits to the back room. INJUN BILL sits, putting the shoes next to him. He takes the bottle and drinks, then pours some into the shoe)

INJUN BILL
I gotta tell ya, George. You've looked better. *(He thinks on this, then starts to laugh. His laugh grows louder and longer)* I'm talking to shoes. I'm talking to a damn pair of shoes! I half expected you to chime right in! *(He laughs more)* George, George, George... I think I gotta get out of this business. I mean... shit, look what it did for you. I reckon I should do like Froggy said... take time to sm... *(He notices the flower from MARTHA's hair on the floor. He picks it up & stares at it for a bit. Finally--)* Ah, what the hell. *(Takes the flower, stares at it for a second, then smells it. It is an overwhelming experience)* Oh my god.

(FROGGY enters)

FROGGY
Bill! You're up on two feet again.

INJUN BILL
Looks like it.

FROGGY
Looky who I found! Bertram Shaw, this here's my good friend... um... Private Filbert Custer.

(DEATH comes to him, shakes his hand)

DEATH
Private Custer, is it?

INJUN BILL
Looks like it.

DEATH
A pleasure.

FROGGY
I was just on my way back when Mr. Shaw here spotted me.

DEATH
He was wearing my hat.

FROGGY
I sure was, I sure was. 'Course I didn't know it was yours at the time, but...

INJUN BILL
Hold up. Do I... were you gonna sell it or some such?

FROGGY
Hey, Martha! I'm back! Bill, you seen Martha?

INJUN BILL
She took some air couple minutes gone. I reckon she'll be back in two ticks.

FROGGY
Well, lemme just pack these eats away. You two get cozy.

(FROGGY heads offstage. DEATH sits)

DEATH
He's a hoot, that one.

INJUN BILL
Froggy? Yeah, he's a kick in the pants all right.

DEATH
He'll talk your ear off though, won't he?

INJUN BILL
That, sir, is a fact.

DEATH
He was telling me a story about a friend of his who killed a man with an apple. An apple, of all things! Can you believe it?

INJUN BILL
Yes. Yes, I can. *(Rises)*

DEATH
Oh. My. What a lovely pair of shoes.

INJUN BILL
Yeah, they're... somethin'.

DEATH
Might I see them?

(BILL just stares at him)

DEATH
I'll give them right back. I promise.

INJUN BILL
Not to piss on your boots, but I went through hell and back to get these. I ain't of a mind to hand 'em over, to you or anyone.

DEATH
I see. I meant no disrespect.

(BILL tips his hat, then turns to go. FROGGY returns)

FROGGY
C'mon over, Bill! Bought me a bottle of Sarsaparilla and I found me three glasses. How's about a snort?

INJUN BILL
I'm 'bout to call it a night.

FROGGY
Come on! This here's the good stuff! Let's... *(sees the shoes)* Smack my ass. Is them what I think them is?

INJUN BILL
Yep.

FROGGY
You did it. You did it, Bill!

INJUN BILL
Well, sorta....

(FROGGY grabs BILL, sits him at the table)

FROGGY
Then we're havin' ourselves a goddamn drink, son! This is... I mean... HOT DAMN!

DEATH
Well, I'm not sure what we're celebrating, but by golly, sometimes it's enough to just celebrate being alive!

FROGGY
Now see! Bert-Ram here gots the right idea! *(FROGGY pours them all sarsaparilla)* Now I should warn ya. Sarsaparilla gives me the butt-trumpets somethin' fierce, but...

INJUN BILL
Jesus, Froggy...

DEATH
Bottoms-Up! And I'm referring to the drinks.

(They laugh, then drink)

FROGGY
Woo! Ain't that sweet.

INJUN BILL
Not bad.

DEATH
Just lovely. So tell me... how did you lads end up in Denver?

FROGGY
Well you might not know it to look at us, Mr. Shaw. But Bill and I met in jail.

DEATH
Is that a fact?

INJUN BILL
Froggy....

FROGGY
Naw, naw. He's all right. Ain't you, Mr. Shaw?

DEATH
I've actually been incarcerated myself.

FROGGY
What?! A nice feller like you?

DEATH
Oh, it's true. You see, I... oh, you don't want to hear that old story.

FROGGY
Sure we do! Don't we, Bill?

INJUN BILL
Honestly, I got no stake in it.

FROGGY
Don't listen to him. He's half-Lakota, half-rattlesnake and half-grizzly bear.

DEATH
Well let's see... this would've been about two years ago. I was in Rawlins... Rawlins, Montana.

FROGGY
Yuh-huh.

DEATH
This was after God burned my family in Atlanta's flames but before I began my bloody march toward the end of days.

FROGGY
Huh. Yeah. You know what, maybe...

DEATH
So there I was in Rawlins and this soldier walks by. A Union Soldier. Now there are few things I hate as much as a Billy Yank, so I... well, I'm not proud of this, but I thumped him. With my bible. Caught him unawares and just....

(DEATH pounds on the table hard. BILL and FROGGY jump)

DEATH
I kept hitting him and hitting him until my precious gospel was covered in his blood. The next thing I know, the constabulary have grabbed me and tossed me in a jail cell. Just me and my blood-soaked bible and...now come to think of it, there was a man in there with me.

FROGGY
Know what? I gotta get supper goin', so...

(FROGGY tries to leave, but DEATH pushes him back into his seat)

DEATH
Well, I'm a chatty fellow. Always have been. I just started to tell this lout my whole story. And do you know what he did, Froggy?

FROGGY
...nope...?

DEATH
He told me his story in return. It turns out this poor man had lost everything too. His one and only friend had been strung up from a pole. And then skinned! And then...now, I know this may be hard to believe, but this man's friend had actually been turned into a pair of shoes! Can you believe it?

INJUN BILL
I know you. You're that crazy priest that....

DEATH
And as he's telling me this story... do you know what happened? *(claps his hands loudly)* Revelation! The truth of God's word made known to me! We two men had been washed in the bloody violence of the world that we might serve the Lord! That, THAT, was the reason why we'd suffered so! Well, as soon as I was released, I set myself to His service. Boys, there's nothing like the feeling of putting a bullet into some hick, and his wife, and his children. Watching them bleed out, then going to their neighbors and doing it again and again. I tell you, there's nothing like it. Nothing in the world.

INJUN BILL
Jesus Christ... you're Death.

DEATH
And you're Injun Bill Picote.

(DEATH quickly grabs FROGGY & slams his head into the table. FROGGY drops)

DEATH
Been a long time.

INJUN BILL
Froggy!

(BILL pulls his knife. DEATH points a gun at him)

DEATH
I hate to ask it, but would you be so kind as to remove your weapons?

(BILL slowly disarms himself)

INJUN BILL
What the hell do you want?

DEATH
Why, to kill every last soul in Denver.

INJUN BILL
What?

DEATH
I've never tried to slaughter a town this big. I don't mind saying, it's taking some doing!

(FROGGY moans. BILL goes to him)

INJUN BIL
Hang in there, son.

FROGGY
....he damn near... cracked my coconut...

INJUN BILL
You're gonna be all right.

DEATH
Well, that's not entirely true.

INJUN BILL
You ain't touchin' him again.

DEATH
William... may I call you William? Surely you can see what this is.

INJUN BILL
Just back off.

DEATH
Providence! God has brought us together for a reason! I mean, to end up in the same place at the same time after all these years...what else could it be?

INJUN BILL
It's just chance, preacher. Dumb, stinkin' chance.

DEATH
Oh, there is no "chance." There is no luck, or coincidence. Everything that has led us to this has been... little miracles in disguise.

INJUN BILL
All right, all right. Don't do nothing crazy.

FROGGY
...too fuckin' late....

INJUN BILL
What exactly is the plan here?

DEATH
The plan? William, the world is ending. There's only one plan. Set it all ablaze, and send the righteous to Heaven. Sing Hallelujah!

(No one says anything. He points his gun at FROGGY)

FROGGY
Hallelujah.

(BILL gets between them)

INJUN BILL
You got no call to kill this man.

DEATH
You may not know this, William, but every time I look into another man's soul, I see his sins manifest. Your friend there is a liar, a glutton and a thief. And you... *(He grabs BILL, staring into his face)* I see every life you've taken. Every lie you've told, and every penny you've stolen. I am the Lord's judgment and I name you guilty.

INJUN BILL
Preacher, I've been a killer damn near all my life, and I can tell you this for free; there ain't no answers in it. Just a long line of people that never got the chance to be something better. I can't never atone for that. Only thing I can do is stop. So I'm asking you, please, put the gun down. Don't make me stop you.

(DEATH shoots INJUN BILL. INJUN BILL stands there for a moment, then drops)

FROGGY
BILL!

(DEATH kicks FROGGY, then goes to BILL)

DEATH
Cursed be he who does the Lord's work remissly; cursed he who holds back his sword from blood - Jeremiah 48:10. *(He points the gun at FROGGY)*

INJUN BILL
...Preacher...

DEATH
Yes?

INJUN BILL
...hey, Preacher...

DEATH
Yes, William? What is it?

INJUN BILL
...you got somethin' on your shirt.

(Beat. DEATH checks his shirt. A large blood stain has formed. He reaches under his jacket and pulls out Quiet Annie)

DEATH
What on Earth?

INJUN BILL
Right in the sweet spot.

(DEATH begins to wobble, and drops his gun)

DEATH
I didn't even feel it.

INJUN BILL
I know. I'm that good.

(DEATH drops to his knees)

DEATH
So... this is what it feels like.

INJUN BILL
Yeah.

DEATH
I didn't think it would be so soon.

INJUN BILL
Hell, I thought it would be sooner.

DEATH
Do you think... everything that's happened to us... was there a reason for it all?

INJUN BILL
Maybe. Don't mean we're meant to know it.

DEATH
Well... I think we're about to find out.

(He falls over dead. FROGGY goes to BILL)

FROGGY
Aw Jesus, Bill.... you hang in there...

INJUN BILL
...don't tell me what to do, ya bastard...

FROGGY
This is a lot of blood.

INJUN BILL
You're tellin' me.

FROGGY
Just keep breathing. I'm gonna get a doctor.

INJUN BILL
Won't do no good. I'm wormfood.

FROGGY
I'll think of something! Just…

(FROGGY rises to leave. INJUN BILL grabs his arm)

FROGGY
You gotta let me do this. I can save you!

INJUN BILL
I think I'm as close to saved as I'm gettin'.

FROGGY
Just stay awake, buddy. Froggy's here.

INJUN BILL
I smelled a flower today, Froggy.

FROGGY
That's real good. Just…

INJUN BILL
It was a hell of a thing. A hell of a thing.

(BILL is fading fast)

FROGGY
You saved me.

INJUN BILL
What're friends for?

FROGGY
C'mon, Bill. You gotta keep your eyes open.

INJUN BILL
Hey. Hey. Froggy?

FROGGY
Yeah?

INJUN BILL
Don't feel bad for me, all right?

FROGGY
...no, no. no....

INJUN BILL
This was a good day.

FROGGY
Bill!

INJUN BILL
This was the best day of my life.

(INJUN BILL dies. FROGGY holds his body and weeps. Lights fade)

Scene 6

MARTHA
(singing)
Let us pause in life's pleasures
And count its many tears,
While we all sup sorrow with the poor;
There's a song that will linger
Forever in our ears;
Oh hard times come again no more.

Tis the song, the sigh of the weary,
Hard Times, hard times, come again no more
Many days you have lingered
Around my cabin door;
Oh hard times come again no more.

(Lights rise. MARTHA & FROGGY at the cemetery. Both are dressed in black)

FROGGY
Thank you for singin' that.

MARTHA
Of course.

FROGGY
Bill liked that song. At least, he told me he liked it. I don't know.

(Beat)

MARTHA
Would you like to keep waiting?

FROGGY
I guess not. Don't know who I thought would show up.

MARTHA
Did he have many friends here?

FROGGY
I don't think he had many friends anywhere.

MARTHA
Oh. *(Beat)* He saved my life, you know. Or rather... he didn't take my life when he could have. It's not exactly the same thing, I suppose, but...

FROGGY
He saved my life too.

MARTHA
Then I guess one might say he was a good man.

FROGGY
I think... for most of his life, he didn't know that was even an option. His conscience came up on his real sudden like.

MARTHA
Then why did you follow him?

FROGGY
I don't know. I liked him.

MARTHA
He liked you too.

FROGGY
Really?

MARTHA
One of the last things he said to me. "Froggy's an all right sort."

FROGGY
He said that?

(She nods. FROGGY is deeply moved by the sentiment)

FROGGY
He was an all right sort too.

(They stand in silence for a bit)

FROGGY
You can go if you want to. You don't have to stay here with me.

MARTHA
I'd like to stay. If you'll have my company.

FROGGY
All right.

MARTHA
Would you like to say something? It might make you feel better.

FROGGY
Well, I wrote out this thing… whaddya call it… a eogo… eulio…

MARTHA
A eulogy?

FROGGY
That's it.

MARTHA
If you'd like to read it, I'll listen.

(He thinks about it)

FROGGY
Naw. It's stupid. And it's real short. Bill wouldn't want me to...

(MARTHA takes his hand)

MARTHA
Jean Phillipe, whatever you have to say, I think he'd want to hear it.

(Beat. FROGGY takes a small piece of paper out of his pocket)

FROGGY
Is there... am I supposed to do something first, or...?

MARTHA
You just have to read it.

FROGGY
All right. *(He reads the paper. As he does, he fights back his own sorrow)* Injun Bill.... Injun Bill Picote... was my friend.

(He puts the paper in his pocket. MARTHA holds him. Lights fade to black)

END OF PLAY

ABOUT THE PLAYWRIGHT

Joseph Zettelmaier is a Michigan-based playwright and four-time nominee for the Steinberg/American Theatre Critics Association Award for best new play, first in 2006 for ALL CHILDISH THINGS, then in 2007 for LANGUAGE LESSONS, in 2010 for IT CAME FROM MARS and in 2012 for DEAD MAN'S SHOES. Other plays include SALVAGE, THE GRAVEDIGGER - A FRANKENSTEIN PLAY, NORTHERN AGGRESSION, DR. SEWARD'S DRACULA, INVASIVE SPECIES, THE SCULLERY MAID, NIGHT BLOOMING, and EBENEZER.

POINT OF ORIGIN won Best Locally Created Script 2002 from the Ann Arbor News, and THE STILLNESS BETWEEN BREATHS also won Best New Play 2005 from the Oakland Press. THE STILLNESS BETWEEN BREATHS and IT

CAME FROM MARS were selected to appear in the National New Play Network's Festival of New Plays. He also co-authored FLYOVER, USA: VOICES FROM MEN OF THE MIDWEST at the Williamston Theatre (Winner of the 2009 Thespie Award for Best New Script). He also adapted CHRISTMAS CAROL'D for the Performance Network.

IT CAME FROM MARS was a recipient of 2009's Edgerton Foundation New American Play Award, and won Best New Script 2010 from the Lansing State Journal. His play DEAD MAN'S SHOES won the Edgerton Foundation New American Play Award in 2011.

Joseph is an Associate Artist at First Folio Shakespeare, an Artistic Ambassador to the National New Play Network, and an adjunct lecturer at Eastern Michigan University, where he teaches Dramatic Composition.

Available Plays by Joseph Zettelmaier

It Came From Mars

Ebeneezer - a Christmas Play

The Gravedigger
A FRANKENSTEIN PLAY
adapted from the novel by Mary Shelly

The Scullery Maid

Dead Man's Shoes

For information about production rights, visit:
www.jzettelmaier.com

More Plays From Sordelet Ink

A Tale of Two Cities
by Christopher M Walsh
adapted from the novel by Charles Dickens

The Count of Monte Cristo
by Christopher M Walsh
adapted from the novel by Alexandre Dumas

The Moonstone
by Robert Kauzlaric
adapted from the novel by Wilkie Collins

The Woman in White
by Robert Kauzlaric
adapted from the novel by Wilkie Collins

Season on the Line
by Shawn Pfautsch
adapted from Herman Melville's Moby-Dick

Hatfield & McCoy
by Shawn Pfautsch

Once A Ponzi Time
by Joe Foust

Eve of Ides
by David Blixt

Visit www.sordeletink.com for more!

NOVELS FROM
SORDELET INK

The Star-Cross'd Series
THE MASTER OF VERONA
VOICE OF THE FALCONER
FORTUNE'S FOOL
THE PRINCE'S DOOM
VARNISH'D FACES & OTHER SHORT STORIES

The Colossus Series
COLOSSUS: STONE & STEEL
COLOSSUS: THE FOUR EMPERORS

and coming 2016
COLOSSUS: WAIL OF THE FALLEN

HER MAJESTY'S WILL
a novel of Wit & Kit

All by bestselling author David Blixt!

And coming in 2016
THE DRAGONTAIL BUTTONHOLE
by Peter Curtis

Visit www.sordeletink.com for more!